'Being an Oxford ghost tour guide of some years standing, I thought I knew everything there is to know about the local ghost scene, but Tom McDonnell's investigative exploration of the city's haunted hot spots is a revelation.'
Jeremy Allen OnBoard issue 177

'An absorbing account of mysterious and unsettling stories from across the ages, right up to the present day. Expertly weaving local history into the narratives, Tom McDonnell also explains how he came by these tales, adding an additional layer of intrigue and allowing the reader to make up their own mind about their veracity.'
Dan Glazebrook Daily Info

AUTOLYCUS BOOKS

First published 2025

Cover Image by Tom McDonnell
Copyright © 2025

Design and typesetting by Joseph Wilkins

ISBN 978-1-0369-3191-9

Autolycus Books
Oxford
OX1 4XB

The general editors of this book have been Marmaduke Postlewaite and Susannah Cartwright.

DEAD BUT AWAKE

A collection of paranormal encounters from the shadows of Oxford

Tom McDonnell

AUTOLYCUS BOOKS
2025

CONTENTS

Introduction: Oxford... A History Of Violence	9
1. The House On Holywell Street	19
2. The Power Of The Ring	25
3. The Man Behind The Door	27
4. Quirky Room Service At The Randolph	35
5. A Sinister Spirit At The Unicorn Theatre	37
6. The Grey Man At The Bear Inn	43
7. The Secrets Of The Cellar Nightclub	47
8. Pembroke College: Room 136	51
9. What Becomes Of The Broken Hearted	61
10. The Ghosts Of Wadham College	67
11. The Linton Road Poltergeists	75
12. Fear And Mischief At The Mitre Inn	77
13. The Ruins Of Godstow	81
14. The Spectres Of The Trout Inn	87
15. Black Jack's Hole	97
16. The Ghosts Of Lincoln College	105
17. The Saxon Tower And The Scared Medium	109
18. A Permanent Resident At The Eastgate Hotel	111
19. Paranormal Activity At The Sheldonian	113
20. Locked Out Of My House	117
21. A Drama At The Playhouse	119
22. The Poltergeist Of St Edmund Hall	123
23. The Phantoms Of Trinity College	127
24. Amy, The Wandering Ghost	135
25. The Wind In The Cemetery	143
26. Malice In The Palace	149
27. The Restless Spirits Of Blackwell's Bookshop	153
28. The Ghosts Of Wytham Woods	157
29. The Jericho Tavern Poltergeists	161
30. Ghosts In The Kitchen, Thieves In The Pantry	163

31. Old Ghosts In The New Theatre	*167*
32. The Haunting Of A Traumatised Mind	*169*
33. Dishwashing Mary	*173*
34. The Castle And The Prison	*175*
35. The Divinity School Pot Boy	*191*
36. Vibes And Frequencies	*195*
37. The Lord Of The Smoke Rings	*201*
38. Slurping Pigs	*203*
39. Blessed George	*205*
40. Brutal George	*211*
41. The Boswell Incident	*219*
42. The Boy With The Lantern	223
43. The Lamentable Tale Of John Crocker	*225*
44. The Man With The Twinkle In His Eye	*235*
45. Treatment Of Dead Enemies	237
46 Hankering For The Glory Days	*241*
47. The Old Lady Of St Giles	*245*
Epilogue	249

Dead but Awake

INTRODUCTION: OXFORD... A HISTORY OF VIOLENCE

The author and renowned philosopher Christopher Hitchens died of oesophageal cancer in 2011, aware that the end was nigh, he made a particularly sobering statement on death.

"It will happen to all of us. At some point you get tapped on the shoulder and told, not just that the party's over- but slightly worse; the party's going on- but you have to leave. And it's going on without you" [1]

Thought provoking words indeed, however Oxford seems to be a place where the party hasn't stopped for scores of long deceased men and women, and although they are seldom invited to the party of life, these restless souls are determined to gatecrash the land of the living.

Oxford's colourful past has left more than just marks in the history books, it has summoned a diverse cast of surprise guests from the spirit world, medieval monks rub shoulders with Victorian butlers, while heartbroken teenagers from the Caroline era drift through the same shadowed streets as headless clergymen, together they form a motley assemblage of spectral wanderers, restless souls bound by place if not time.

The University of Oxford is the oldest in England and the third oldest in Europe, the world-renowned institution is made up of thirty-nine colleges, a grand graduation hall and countless libraries and lecture halls.

But beyond the academic prestige lies a darker side, from ancient university buildings to taverns, town houses, and cobbled alleyways, Oxford is steeped with stories of the supernatural, paranormal activity seems woven into the very fabric of the place.

With its cosy pubs and open green spaces, Oxford gives the impression of a peaceful haven. But behind the serene façade lies a history steeped in conflict. Over the centuries, the city has witnessed its share of bloodshed, especially during the English Civil War, when Royalists and Parliamentarians clashed over the right to govern the country. It is certainly worth a brief exploration of this conflict to contextualise Oxford's role in the war.

OXFORD AND THE ENGLISH CIVIL WAR

King Charles I inherited his father's unwavering belief in the divine right of kings, he was determined to rule with absolute power. This inflexible mindset, coupled with his refusal to entertain opposing views, quickly earned him many enemies.

History suggests that the king would have benefited from the counsel of financial advisors. He was disastrously inept with money, his extravagant spending on art alone nearly crippled the crown's finances. Yet it wasn't just his misguided economic decisions that raised concerns. His personal life also stirred public outrage. But the king marched to the beat of his own drum, in a nation still reeling from the memory of the Gunpowder Plot, Charles chose to marry Henrietta Maria, a Roman Catholic, provoking widespread unease.

Beyond his controversial marriage and lavish spending, Charles repeatedly alienated Parliament. His policies of arbitrary taxation bred deep resentment, and when met with resistance, he frequently dissolved Parliament without its consent. Unpopular wars against France, Spain, and even Scotland further soured relations with both Parliament and the public.

Tensions reached a boiling point on 22 November 1641, when Parliament presented Charles with the Grand Remonstrance, a document which listed their grievances since his accession. Around the same time, news of a rebellion in Ireland reached London. Parliament, fearing the King might use a raised army to suppress them instead of the Irish, sought to pass a militia bill that would place military power in their hands. When pressed to surrender control of the army, Charles famously declared, "By God, not for an hour."

Increasingly desperate and fearing the possible impeachment of his Catholic queen, Charles made a bold and reckless move. He ordered the arrest of five members of the Commons and one from the House of Lords on charges of treason. He personally led over four hundred men into Parliament to carry out the arrests only to discover that his targets had already fled. The fuse was thus lit for civil war.

With London no longer safe, Charles fled the capital and, after wandering from city to city, he eventually arrived in Oxford which, for the next four years, would function as the royal court of England, though it remained under near-constant siege. In 1646, Cromwell's Roundheads successfully stormed the city. Charles escaped, apparently disguised as a servant, but he was soon captured.

In 1648, after several bloody skirmishes, Charles was put on trial. He stood accused of placing his own interests above those of the nation. Stubborn to the end, he refused to acknowledge the authority of the court or accept responsibility. Found guilty of treason, he was given just three days to settle his affairs before his execution.

On 30 January 1649, Charles I was beheaded on Tower Hill. After the fatal blow from the axe, the executioner held up the king's head before dropping it into a crowd of soldiers. Some of whom cut locks of his hair and tore pieces from his blood-soaked garments, a savvy move given that these gruesome keepsakes would later fetch high prices as morbid souvenirs.

The aftermath of the Civil War brought lasting scars to Oxford. Many of Cromwell's soldiers were Puritans who despised Catholicism, and their iconoclasm left the city's sacred art in ruins. Statues of saints in New College Chapel were smashed beyond recognition. A statue of the Virgin Mary above the University Church door remains marked by bullet holes to this day and stained-glass windows in Christ Church Chapel were shattered.

Given this violent purge of Catholic heritage, it is perhaps no surprise that many of Oxford's most persistent ghosts were men of the Catholic faith.

Tales of ghosts from the English civil war are rife in Oxford but its legacy of violence reaches back much further. Two devastating "town versus gown" riots in the 13th and 14th centuries and the infamous St. Brice's Day Massacre on 13 November 1002, stand as stark reminders of the city's turbulent past.

THE TOWN VS GOWN RIOTS

When students poured into Oxford from 1167 onwards, their presence quickly became a source of tension. Often indulging in drunkenness and loutish behaviour, they earned a reputation for mischief that, some locals might argue, persists to this day. But it wasn't just their rowdiness that frustrated the townspeople, between the 13th and 19th centuries, students enjoyed significant financial privileges that bred deep resentment. They paid reduced prices for goods, were exempt from local taxes, and operated outside the jurisdiction of lay authorities.

But these were dark and volatile times. A careless insult from an arrogant student could quickly incite a street brawl and on occasion, even trigger a full-blown riot.

In 1209, a number of Oxford students thought it might be a hoot to dabble with archery, unfortunately, their aim was as bad as their judgment and a local girl was killed by a stray arrow, the townsfolk of Oxford were understandably furious and violence erupted, fearing for their lives, many students and tutors fled the city, seeking refuge nearly a hundred miles away in a small town called Cambridge, and just like that, the foundations were laid for Oxford's most famous rival.

Another violent clash, The Saint Scholastica Day Riot, erupted in 1355, sparked by that time-honoured catalyst for trouble, an argument over alcohol.

On Tuesday, 10 February, two Oxford scholars, Walter Spryngeheuse and Roger de Chesterfield, swaggered into the wonderfully named Swindlestock Tavern on Fish Street (now St Aldate's) and ordered some cups of wine, displeased with the quality of the booze, they complained loudly to the landlord, John Groidon. A heated exchange followed, culminating in the offending drink being thrown over the landlord's head. The scholars then proceeded to physically assault him, a grave mistake, as Groidon was well-liked by the townspeople.

The Mayor of Oxford, outraged on behalf of the landlord, demanded that the university chancellor have the students arrested. But the mayor's stern condemnation provoked a backlash: a group of students, loyal to their fellow scholars, rallied in defiance. The situation escalated rapidly when the angry students assaulted the mayor himself.

Furious townsfolk rang the bells of St Martin's Church to rally reinforcements, and soon all-out war was declared. A small militia of thugs rode in from Abingdon, six miles away, to support the townspeople. the Abingdon mob brandished black flags as they galloped into the city, an ominous symbol of their intentions.

Over the course of three days, at least sixty-three students and thirty townsfolk were killed in the ensuing chaos. Accounts describe horrifying scenes, tutors scalped by locals, disembowelled students staggering through the streets, clutching their intestines and begging for aid. According to tradition, so much blood ran along the High Street that the Pope ordered the ground to be reconsecrated.

In the aftermath, the town was found to be at fault. As penance, every February 10th, the mayor and town councillors were required to march bareheaded to the university church and pay a fine of one penny for each slain scholar, totalling 5 shillings and 3 pence. This ritual continued until 1825, when a defiant mayor refused to participate. The symbolic feud wasn't formally resolved until 1955, when the centuries-old "town and gown" rift was finally laid to rest.

Even today, violence flares up between the students and the locals each February, but the pitchforks are for now set aside, and the action takes place in the annual 'town vs. gown' boxing event.

The Saint Brice's Day Massacre

Two hundred years before the St Scholastica Day riot, a largely forgotten but remarkably brutal event shook England: the St Brice's Day massacre. This nationwide bloodshed occurred during the reign of King Æthelred, a time when England was plagued by relentless Viking raids of legendary barbarity. By 1002, many Danes had settled peacefully across the country, but rising tensions reached a breaking point when the King was informed of a Danish plot against his life.

What followed was a grim act of ethnic cleansing. On Æthelred's orders, all Danes living in England were to be attacked and killed at dawn on 13 November.

Across the country, Danish settlers were slaughtered in their sleep. In one chilling discovery, an excavation outside

St John's College in March 2008 unearthed the remains of nearly forty Danes. Their skeletons bore signs of extreme violence, smashed skulls, stab wounds to the pelvis and spine, injuries consistent with a sudden dawn attack. Many appear to have been killed while fleeing or still in their beds, as defensive wounds typical of hand-to-hand combat, such as lacerations on the arms and shoulders, were largely absent.

Some of the Oxford based Danes desperately sought refuge in St Frideswide's Church, located on the site where Christ Church now stands. But even this house of God offered no protection, the townspeople set fire to the church, burning those inside alive.[2]

In early 2025, an American PhD student told me there had been whispers of ghostly Vikings seen wandering near the excavation site. Although I gave her my business card and she seemed eager to share more, I've sadly heard nothing since.

With Oxford's historic backdrop of violence and murder, it's of little surprise that there's been a great number of ghostly sightings reported in the county. Within the pages of this book, I have given my take on some of the better-known Oxford legends, but what I believe sets *Dead but Awake* apart from other books on Oxford's supernatural history, is the unprecedented number of first-hand accounts that I have managed to collect, I have also collected a great number of second hand accounts which have never before been published, I have interviewed people from all walks of life, night porters, college archivists, summer school students, hoteliers and bar staff.

However, it would be remiss of me not to acknowledge the work of earlier authors whose research has preserved numerous first-hand accounts, providing a valuable foundation for my own research. In particular, I am indebted to the works of John Richardson and my dear friend Marilyn Yurdan. The research papers and support of Nuala Young and Eva Wagner have also been invaluable, and I am grateful to Magnus Macfarlane for his careful editing of those papers. Iain Stevenson's knowledge and enthusiasm for this project have likewise been of immense help, I must also thank Simon Image for introducing me to some of the classic Oxford ghost stories which I have re-examined.

Unfortunately, just before the scheduled interviews, two individuals who had initially agreed to share their experiences changed their minds. The events they'd endured were simply too traumatic for them to revisit. While I was admittedly frustrated by their last-minute jitters, their wishes were, of course, to be respected. That said, one of the stories, involving a group of Buddhist monks performing an exorcism in a house on Holywell Street, particularly piqued my curiosity. Having already conducted research on another property on the same street, I was eager to explore whether the reported manifestations might somehow be linked to skirmishes that took place there during the parliamentarian siege of 1646, perhaps the future will give up the ghost and I may find myself writing a second volume.

My Personal Interests in The Paranormal

When I was five years old, my school report noted a 'disturbing interest in the paranormal.' I would argue, however, that it was a healthy curiosity, I have also spent many years studying witchcraft folklore, if you need any further assurance that you're in good hands, I should mention, at the risk of sounding like I come from a family of eccentrics, that some relatives on my mother's side not only believed in ghosts but also claimed to have seen them. On occasion, they even went out of their way to contact these spirits.

In this book, I will also share accounts of strange events that I have personally witnessed.

So I suggest that you dim the lights slightly, fill your glass with your favourite tipple, make yourself comfortable and ready yourself for an expedition into the shadowy realm of the supernatural, where I will share the fruits of my labour, the accounts that I've collected... stories of the dead... dead, yet somehow... still awake...

Dead but Awake

1.
THE HOUSE ON HOLYWELL STREET

In December 2016, I was offered the opportunity to manage a quaint bed and breakfast, a property on Holywell Street, a lovely spot in the city of Oxford, although I was undeniably tempted, several commitments sadly prevented me from taking up the offer. The charming house, which dates back to the 1530s, seems to be held together by gnarled wooden beams, twisted and weathered by time. The steps of the old staircase are equally contorted, and the rooms are arranged so eccentrically that the layout would baffle a modern-day structural engineer.

Stu and Carrie, the couple who had run the guest house for over a decade, generously gave me two hours of their time to walk me through the many responsibilities involved in managing the place. After a tour of the house, we sat in the living quarters, where I found myself surrounded by curious antiques and old-fashioned teapots. It was there that I decided to broach the subject of ghosts, I'd heard rumours over the years that their guest house might be haunted, surprisingly, Carrie didn't flinch at my questions. In fact, she spoke in detail about the strange happenings she had witnessed at the house. But before I share these accounts with the reader, I feel it's important to first describe the topography of the house.

Holywell Street is a charming area with student accommodation occupying most of the street. There's also a concert hall, a sushi restaurant, a tuck shop, and The Kings Arms, a 17th century public house.

The entire street was built on the site of a sprawling Augustinian friary, which fell victim to King Henry VIII's dissolution of the monasteries in the 1530s. While the king's legislation was intended to seize assets from the monasteries for the benefit of the state, the Augustinian friary was, in fact, an impoverished house in a state of squalor.

Opposite the guesthouse stands New College, a truly magnificent institution built on the site of a plague pit. Despite its name, it was established in the 14th century. William of Wykeham, the Bishop of Winchester, founded the college as a training ground for priests after the Black Death had wiped out a third of the nation's clergy. Given this history, I speculated that the guesthouse might be haunted by the restless spirit of a displaced friar, forever resentful of his eviction from the friary. Or perhaps it was the ghost of a plague victim. It would transpire that I was completely off track.

Carrie told me that not long after they moved into the property, she started to notice a series of strange incidents occurring around the house. At first, some were so subtle she barely registered them, but as time passed and she spent more time there, the occurrences became harder to ignore. Occasionally, Carrie would hear a strange humming echoing throughout the house. At other times she would catch the sound of someone whistling what sounded like an old melody. One room in particular, tucked away on the first floor, seemed to be a constant hub of persistent and unsettling activity.

Carrie mentioned that after making the beds and tending to other chores, she would often return to this room only to find a depression on one of the beds she had just made, as if someone had come in and sat down. Carrie also noticed that a small wooden chair, which she always positioned against the wall, would inexplicably be moved, pushed forward by about four inches each time.

Carrie explained that it was typically when she was alone in the house that she felt a distinct presence, as if

The living room in the haunted guest house.
{Photograph} Tom McDonnell

someone else was in the house with her, it must be noted however, that at no point did Carrie ever feel threatened by this entity. In fact, quite the opposite, she told me that she found its presence strangely comforting.

As is often the case with old buildings, maintenance issues inevitably arise. Stu and Carrie discovered a damp problem on one of the walls. While the damp didn't make its way into the room with the moving chairs and disturbed duvets, it did affect a small passageway connecting the breakfast room to the kitchen on the ground floor. Naturally concerned about the damp, the couple arranged to have the wooden panelled wall in the passageway temporarily removed for a thorough inspection.

Fortunately, the guest house is owned by Merton college and as landlord they were obliged to supply the

Passageway in the house on Holywell Street where the skeleton was discovered.
{Photograph} Tom McDonnell

workmen without charge.

As the workmen removed the wooden panelled wall, a wave of shock swept across their faces. Behind it, they uncovered a human skeleton. On closer inspection, they discovered a sword had been thrust right through its body. Any concerns Stu and Carrie had about the damp suddenly seemed trivial, now, their guest house would become the scene of a murder investigation.

The police were called and both the body and the sword were taken for analysis in a laboratory. The results revealed that the man behind the wall hadn't been the victim of a recent murder; forensics traced his death back to the late 1640s. It also turned out that the sword dated to the early 1600s. It's likely no coincidence that the man was killed around the same time Cromwell's troops successfully stormed the city in 1646.

It is therefore assumed, with good reason, that the murdered man was a royalist Cavalier, though it remains unclear as to why the sword wasn't removed, I did uncover something interesting: that even in the blood-soaked days of the 17th century, there was an unwritten code of honour to not 'finish off' an injured, unarmed man. It's possible that he was left to bleed to death, as for why his body was sealed behind the wall, that remains a mystery.

The skeleton was taken to the Pitt-Rivers Museum, where it was cleaned and examined. According to Carrie, as soon as the body was removed, the whistling, the humming, the rumpling of the bed sheets and the rearranging of the chairs all stopped. It seems that, at last, this spirit has found some peace.[3]

Dead but Awake

2.
THE POWER OF THE RING

Oxford's Radcliffe Square is home to many iconic buildings and landmarks which, according to numerous tour guides, have inspired some of the greatest works of fantasy literature. The two towers of All Souls College are said to have influenced Tolkien's depiction of the towers in *The Lord of the Rings*, while an old lamp post on St Mary's Passage is often linked to the one in *The Lion, the Witch and the Wardrobe* by C.S. Lewis. These connections are admittedly tenuous—but in the summer of 2024, I was told of a strange occurrence involving that very lamp post … and a ring.

The following incident was witnessed by a couple who had recently moved to Oxford, Sanchari and Rohan. What follows is the account, as told from Sanchari's perspective.

"It was around 11pm to 11.30pm in the month of February, 2024 when I and my partner went for a night-walk around the city centre, we reached the Bodleian library from the main road, it was almost empty with a van parked in the distance behind the library. As the square was almost desolate, we decided to return to the city centre but just as we reached near the lamp post beside the University church, I could see a third shadow falling in front of us, illuminated by the street light, the phantom shadow was directly in the middle of our shadows. It felt like someone was rushing towards us and l immediately got alarmed thinking it must be a drunkard or someone trying to attack us, I promptly turned back. But I could see no one around us, the incident gave me a chill."

The identity of the shadowy figure that rushed at the couple remains unknown. However, there may have been a reason Sanchari was particularly vulnerable to aggressive spirits on that specific night, as she informs us.

"I always wear my red coral stone ring on my right hand which has some spiritual significance in India. While returning that night I realised that I had left my ring at home."

According to astrological tradition, Sanchari's belief in the ring holds some significance, for those who wear Red Coral, also known as Moonga, are said to be protected from the wrath of malicious enemies and evil spirits.[4]

3.
THE MAN BEHIND THE DOOR

On the morning of 29 June 2021, I met with two students from Jesus College, Alfie C and Alfie W.H. We were also joined by fellow ghost enthusiast and Jesus college alumnus, Iain Stevenson. The purpose of our meeting was to discuss one of the most intriguing reports of paranormal activity I've ever encountered, the ghost of Staircase 17 at Jesus College.

This story unfolds during the COVID pandemic in 2021, a surreal and unforgettable time to be a student at Oxford.

In his first year at Jesus College, Alfie W. H. lived in the third quadrangle on Staircase 17. A bathroom separated his room from Room 11, which had been assigned to his friend Raph. However, due to the Covid pandemic, many students were placed in accommodation outside the college grounds. Raph was assigned student housing in Cowley, just over a mile from the city centre—along with their mutual friend, Alfie C.

One morning, well into Hilary term, Alfie W.H. was standing in the third quadrangle when he noticed that the windows of Room 11 were wide open. At first, he assumed the cleaner had simply forgotten to close them. However, Raph hadn't stayed in college since before Christmas, meaning the room had been unoccupied for months. It seemed unlikely that a cleaner would bother with an empty room. Alfie W.H. concluded that perhaps a pigeon had flown in and thought little more of it.

It's important to note that during the pandemic, students were only permitted to return to their rooms when authorised by the college, and they returned in staggered intervals to prevent the spread of the virus. Raph wasn't officially allowed back into Jesus College until Trinity term. Without keys from the porters, it would have been impossible for him to access Room 11. We can therefore say with confidence that Raph had not returned to his room and could not have been the one to leave the windows open.

During Trinity term, Alfie W.H. noticed once again that the windows of Room 11 were wide open. He made a mental note to mention it to Raph who was still living in Cowley and hadn't been into his college room for several months. It occurred to Alfie that if a pigeon had flown in, the room could be in quite a state.

A few nights later, Raph and Alfie C unofficially returned to the college to visit some friends. Since they hadn't officially checked in, they had no access to their rooms and did not have their keys. Around 11 p.m, a few students were gathered in the foyer area of the third quadrangle, near the JCR at the base of Staircase 17. It's worth noting that no one had been drinking heavily or using drugs, Alfie C later admitted to having just one small beer.

Alfie W.H. joined the group of students, Raph, Alfie C and Olly, and mentioned that the windows to Raph's room had been swinging open since Hilary term. The group joked about the possibility of squatters living in Room 11. As they laughed, they all happened to glance up toward the window from the third quad, and in that moment, they noticed a sudden change. The light in the room seemed to brighten for just a few seconds, almost like a flash, before fading again.

Although they couldn't access Room 11, the two Alfie's and Raph decided to head upstairs to investigate. At this point, the mood was still light-hearted, with plenty of banter. Raph was the target of good-natured teasing, with comments like, "There's definitely something going on in your room, mate."

When they reached the top of the stairs, they passed Alfie W.H.'s room and turned left toward Room 11. As they approached the room, Alfie C joked, "It's probably just a cleaner—but wouldn't it be funny if we found a squatter living in Raph's room?".

When they reached Room 11, the group began messing around, banging on the door and calling out, "Is anyone in there?" Amid the laughter, Alfie W.H. suddenly thought he heard a faint noise from inside. Curious, he scrambled up, gripping the doorframe with his fingers, and tried to peer through the small windowpane set into the top of the door. Alfie W.H.'s grip slipped on the first attempt, his feet scraping noisily against the door. On the second try, he managed to haul himself up and peer through the window. What he saw to the left of the room gave him the shock of his life: a man was standing inside, side-on, next to the door, facing directly toward the group. The moment Alfie W.H. caught sight of the top of the man's head, he dropped down instantly, visibly shaken. Struggling to process what he'd just seen, he told the others there was someone in the room. At first, Alfie C assumed he was joking. After about thirty seconds of back-and-forth and still convinced it was some kind of prank, he decided to climb up and take a look for himself, the ledge beneath the windowpane is extremely narrow, offering barely enough space to grip. Alfie C managed to pull himself up for just a second, long enough to peer through the glass. As he glanced to the left, he too saw the man. The figure stood in a slightly hunched posture, arms crossed, poised as if listening intently to the students on the other side of the door. Alfie C observed that the man didn't appear frightened, but there was a slight recoil in his stance.

He dropped down with his heart pounding, feeling "pretty damned scared", he thought to himself 'this is too much for me, there is someone actually in the room', as the group tried to gather themselves, Alfie W.H, in a state of utter disbelief, said aloud "there is someone actually in the room, are we tripping?"

It is important to highlight that Alfie W.H did not describe the appearance of the man to Alfie C before he peered through the window pane, they both however gave the same description, that of a young male aged between 15- 20, wearing a white vest, his arms folded with his hands placed on his shoulders, his face was pale white and his black hair combed to one side. They both agreed that the man appeared to have a modern hairstyle.

The students agreed it was best to call the porter. When he arrived, he unlocked the door to Room 11, and the group entered together. The lights were still off but mysteriously; the window was now closed. Once inside, both Alfie's quickly reached the same unsettling conclusion: there simply wasn't enough space for anyone to have been standing where they'd seen the man. They both claimed the man had been standing between the door and the wall on the left-hand side. However, the wall would have needed to be at least thirty centimetres farther to the left for there to be enough space for anyone to stand there.

About half an hour after the sighting, the bemused porter returned to his office, while the two Alfie's and Raph made their way back down the stairs to the foyer area. Alfie C stood near a drain at the entrance to Staircase 17, directly beneath the window of Room 11. Alfie W.H. stood roughly ten metres away from the entrance. Both were trying to process what they had just witnessed; Alfie C began recounting the sighting to another student, Jess who was lingering in the foyer. It's worth noting that, at the time, he had a large 660ml bottle of beer tucked into the oversized front pocket of his jacket. The pocket stretched across the front like an apron, with only the neck of the bottle visible, the rest of it firmly wedged and supported by the fabric, As Alfie C was recounting the sighting, he was suddenly interrupted by a sharp, forceful crash that echoed across the foyer—loud enough for everyone to hear, including Alfie W.H, who was standing some distance away.

The 660ml bottle, which had been firmly wedged in the front pocket of Alfie C's jacket, had smashed violently on the ground near the drain. Strangely, no one had seen it fall. It hadn't slipped or tumbled; yet seemed to have hit the ground with a sudden, deliberate force.

Raph immediately asked Alfie C to check his pocket for any holes, there were none. Meanwhile, Olly and Jess glanced upward, as if the bottle might have been hurled from above. The intensity of the smash suggested it hadn't just fallen; it was as if the bottle had been thrown from a great height.

So, we have five people stood in a circle, all facing each other, yet not one of them saw the bottle fall. [5] And all five agreed that the intensity of the crash seemed completely out of proportion to the short distance between Alfie C's pocket and the ground, Alfie C told me that his friend Olly, a law student, had never been even the slightest bit superstitious. But Olly himself admitted that the prime reason he was now open to the possibility of something supernatural was the incident with the bottle.

During his first year at Jesus College, Alfie C lived on the third floor, just below Room 11. He told me that he always felt the place had a genuinely unsettling atmosphere, especially when walking through the dim corridors to use the bathroom late at night.

In an effort to make sense of this sighting, I began researching the history of Jesus College, and particularly the third quadrangle.

Jesus College was founded in 1571 by Queen Elizabeth

I, at the request of Hugh Price, the treasurer of St David's Cathedral in Pembrokeshire. A former Oxford student, Price was eager to establish a place of learning in Oxford for Welsh clergymen. For the first 350 years, all members of the college were Welsh, and many of today's students also share Welsh heritage. Both Alfie's, in fact, have Welsh roots.

The third quadrangle is located on the north side of the college, where stables once stood in the 1700s. In 1904, the stables were destroyed by fire. The ruins were cleared, and a gateway to Ship Street was created. Within two years, new buildings were erected on the site, effectively forming what is now the third quadrangle. Completed in 1907, these buildings originally housed the college's chemistry laboratories. However, since 1945, they have served as student accommodation—including Staircase 17. This means that the apparition was witnessed in a relatively modern setting: an early twentieth-century room, built no earlier than 1907.

While examining the archives of Jesus College, I discovered that a former principal, David William Hughes, had committed suicide in 1817. I found this particularly interesting, as he shared a surname with one of the Alfie's—a striking coincidence, given that Alfie's surname is a blend of both his parents' surnames. But the tragic principal is clearly not the spectre said to haunt Room 11. He killed himself at the age of sixty-seven and, based on surviving portraits, appears to have been a large, rotund man.

The description of the apparition does, however, bear some resemblance to a former Jesus College student who tragically took his own life outside of Oxford in more recent years. Out of respect for his friends and family, I have chosen not to pursue that line of investigation.

I did consider the possibility that the man behind the

The window paned door in Jesus College, which the mysterious man hid behind
{Photograph} Tom McDonnell

door was a squatter. Several security staff at the Bodleian Library have told me about homeless students with drug issues secretly sleeping there overnight. If the man in Room 11 was indeed a squatter, he would have needed to be extremely agile to climb through a very small window—and remarkably bold to make his way across the college rooftops. Still, desperate people will go to great lengths to find warmth and shelter. But even if he was a squatter, that still wouldn't explain the incident with the flying bottle.

So, for the time being, it seems the identity of the strange man in Room 11 will remain unknown, another curious chapter consigned to the archive of unsolved mysteries.

Dead but Awake

4.
QUIRKY ROOM SERVICE AT THE RANDOLPH

On 11 June 2023, I met up once again with Oxford tour guide and all-round top ghost enthusiast, Iain Stevenson, we had a couple of pints in the Morse bar of the Randolph hotel, Iain told me about a strange incident which happened to an English couple who were staying at the Randolph not long after the covid pandemic in late 2020, the Randolph is a five star hotel, due to the covid travel restrictions the couple had managed to get a good deal, business wasn't exactly booming at this time, the couple however got the surprise of their lives when they ordered room service.

Only a few minutes had passed since they'd ordered a sandwich when there was a knock at the door. While the speed of the room service was surprising, what truly startled them was the appearance of the middle-aged attendant, dressed in attire that looked far more suited to the 1930s or 40s than the present day.

The man told the couple he had just come from an air base in Kenley. Then, without warning, he opened his shirt to reveal an indentation on his chest, a wound he claimed was the result of a champagne cork accident, sustained when he'd opened the bottle clumsily. The guests, dumbstruck, could only stare, the attendant then left and went on his merry way, when the guests mentioned this incident to other members of staff, no one seemed to know who the mysterious figure was. It is however, particularly intriguing that the man claimed to have just come from Kenley Air Base, and that he was dressed in a uniform that seemed to belong to an era when Vera Lynn topped the charts and George Formby lit up cinema screens.

Until my conversation with Iain, I had never heard of RAF Kenley. I soon discovered it had been a key Royal Air Force airfield during the Second World War—one of three major fighter stations tasked with defending London from the skies.

18 August 1940, later dubbed "The Hardest Day", marked the moment the RAF endured its most devastating losses during the Battle of Britain. As the Luftwaffe launched a ferocious assault, sixty-eight aircraft were torn from the skies. RAF Kenley bore the brunt of the onslaught: two of its three hangars were reduced to rubble, buildings lay in ruins, and ten aircraft were annihilated on the ground. The airfield, once a stronghold of defence, had been left obliterated.[6]

Could it be the case that our eccentric hotel worker perished on that fateful day in 1940, yet returns to his old job, hankering for simpler times, when the world was not at war, and dodging a champagne cork, as opposed to a bomb, was the most dangerous aspect of his day-to-day duties.[7]

5.
A SINISTER SPIRIT AT THE UNICORN THEATRE

The Unicorn Theatre is based in a stone structure nestled lengthwise in-between two earlier buildings; The Checker built around 1260 to the east and the abbey barn (later the bakehouse) to the west.

The roof is butted against two existing gable walls at either end. It was reconstructed with an impressive roof in the fifteenth century, probably for domestic use. It's assumed to have been used as a granary prior to the dissolution of the monasteries but was likely returned to domestic use thereafter and by the nineteenth century it had been partitioned into three cottages.

The Friends of Abingdon acquired the building in the 1940s, The theatre conversion dates from 1952-3, it is a delightful 92-seater theatre, and the stage and gallery were designed very much in the Elizabethan style,

The concept of the Unicorn Theatre was the brainchild of Alan Kitching, who experienced a lightbulb moment in 1952 while strolling with his wife through the ruins of Abingdon Abbey. They had each paid six pence for a self-guided tour, but what they found was far from grand: in Kitching's own words, "a more or less derelict building, with four (rather scabby) walls and a tolerably weatherproof roof." Today, the theatre stands worlds apart from that humble beginning.[8]

The Unicorn theatre may be a charming place now, but unsettling reports tell of a malignant presence haunting its halls, I have heard several accounts from someone who worked there in 2019.

I was told that upon entering the cellar people would feel like throwing up, one person described it as "ghost induced sickness".

When a temporary cinema screen was fitted, an invisible force tore it down, it was likely the same violent entity which winded a member of staff by punching him in the chest.

Often and usually at 9.45pm, someone or something reportedly hammers on the inside of the ceiling of what was the old monastery.[9]

It is of little surprise that paranormal investigations take place at the theatre on a regular basis, but who is this violent entity who can apparently leap in the air and smash their fists on the ceiling, delving through old newspaper articles I came across a 19th century newspaper report of a mischievous spectre which roamed around this particular area of Abingdon and seems to fit the bill.

The following report is from *The Faringdon Advertiser and Vale of the Whitehorse Gazette*: Saturday 22 September 1888.

> **"The Conduit Ghost.** An alarming story reaches me this week to the effect that a ghost has been seen in the vicinity of the Lonesome Tree, Conduit fields. Whether the apparition is merely re-appearance of the "Ock Street ghost," which caused so much uneasiness among the poorer inhabitants, and whose vagaries were graphically described by a contemporary a few years ago, we are unable to say. It may be that the perturbed spirit, which at that time made its presence known by violently thumping the walls and doors of one the vacant alms houses in Ock Street, has at last come out for a little exercise, the ghost in question being observed to jump about like a grass-hopper and to reach the branches of lofty elm tree at one bound. It has the appearance

of countryman, wears long beard and a smock, but is a veritable spring-heel-jack, scaling the road with extraordinary agility and then vanishing out of sight, Great excitement prevails among the juveniles, several of whom claim the distinction of being eye-witnesses, and on Sunday night the boys congregated in Park road in such large numbers to "see the ghost" that the services at St. Michael's Church were considerably interrupted by the noise they made."[10]

The report claims that in 1888, Abingdon was apparently terrorised by a remarkably athletic ghost—possibly the same spectre who had "caused so much uneasiness" among the town's poorer residents a few years

The Unicorn Theatre, a pretty place with a troublesome spirit.
{Photograph} Tom McDonnell

earlier. The local kids were clearly enthralled by the ghost but if the rest of the townsfolk had hoped for respite, they were surely disappointed, for *The Henley Advertiser* reported that the ghost had apparently returned to cause more mayhem in 1891.

> "Abingdon. A Ghost Scare. Once more is the peace of mind of the poorer townsfolk disturbed by the supposed reappearance of the Ock Street ghost, which caused so much alarm a few years ago. This time the ghost is said to have quartered itself in West Saint Helen Street in a passage nearly opposite the old Wheatsheaf Inn, and for the last fortnight the street at this spot has every evening been thronged with a crowd of excited men, women, and boys. The occupants of the small tenements up the court in question declare they get no extravagant ghost, for it delights in throwing coal and coke and even young potatoes through the cottagers' windows. Almost every tenant in the yard has suffered in this way. We cannot but ridicule the idea that such damage is caused by a supernatural agency. It is, however, certainly strange that the missiles should come as they do from all directions and apparently from over the roofs of the houses and quite regardless of the presence of a numerous company of watchers. Ladders have been obtained and the roofs searched in the vicinity, on the supposition that someone was concealed, but with no result. The police, too, have kept watch, and they went so far as to arrest on suspicion the supposed ghost in the person of one of the tenants of the court, named Alfred Carter. He was,

however, released for want of evidence, and in, consequence, perhaps, of the fact that whilst in the lock-up the window smashing had in no way abated."[11]

Could it be that the violent spectre who wreaks havoc at the Unicorn theatre is the spring heeled jack who disturbed the peace in nearby Ock street back in the 1800s, it's a tempting theory and perhaps another paranormal investigation may uncover the truth, then again, a friend did attend a seance at the theatre and nothing remotely weird happened, although that may support my belief that some people are more in tune with the paranormal than others.

Dead but Awake

6.
THE GREY MAN AT THE BEAR INN

Until around 2003, the Oxford Tourist Information Centre was tucked inside a disused Victorian schoolhouse conveniently located next to the main bus station and even more conveniently, it shared the building with a pub. I worked part-time at the information desk back then and, on more than one occasion, found myself 'researching local culture' over a lunchtime Guinness. As Oscar Wilde so perfectly put it: "I can resist everything except temptation".

Around this time, Eva Wagner—an Austrian-born, Oxford-based tour guide—was running ghost tours from the visitor's centre. She and a fellow guide Nuala Young have kindly shared the following story with me, one that centres around The Bear Inn on Blue Boar Street, just a stone's throw from Oxford's city centre.

The Bear Inn dates to around 1242 and is arguably the oldest pub in Oxford. It's also one of the city's smallest, a charming spot that's well worth a visit.

Eva recounted a tale from the late 1980s involving a landlord who lived in a flat above the pub with his wife and their four-year-old son. One afternoon, while his wife was out shopping, the landlord took the opportunity to clean out the basement. Their son remained upstairs in the flat, safely behind a stair gate to keep him from wandering or falling down the stairs.

As the landlord sorted through the basement, he came across a small wall cupboard. Curious, he pulled the door open—and that's when things took a strange turn, he received quite a shock when a large number of bones spilled out on to the floor, on closer inspection, the Landlord saw that the bones, which were covered in grey sludge, were human remains, as he hastily collected the

The haunted Bear Inn, possibly Oxfords oldest pub.
{*Photograph*} *Tom McDonnell*

bones and placed them into a rubbish bag, he suddenly realised that he wasn't alone in the basement, to his great surprise his son was stood next to him and began to assist him with putting the bones away, the landlord asked the boy if "Mummy had come back?" to which the boy replied "no".

The father, understandably perplexed, then asked the boy how he had managed to come down the stairs, with the safety gate locked, the boy said, "The Grey man helped me".

The Landlord suddenly suspected that burglars were on the prowl, however, after racing into the house, he discovered that nothing had been disturbed, and the safety gate was still locked.

The landlord then turned to his son and asked him "What Grey man?"

The boy's response was chilling: "The Grey Man who plays with me when you're not there"

According to research notes compiled by Eva and Nuala in the early 1990's, a graveyard had existed below the foundation of the Bear Inn in the 8th century. [12]

It's no surprise that Eva chose to include this fascinating story in her ghost tour. One evening, while leading a group along Deadman's Walk, a path that runs along the northern edge of Christ Church meadow, she shared the tale of the Grey Man. As she finished, a man in the group spoke up. Not only had he worked at The Bear Inn, but he claimed to have been present when the bones were discovered. Naturally, Eva was intrigued. She asked him to recount what had happened.

He explained that, while the landlord's young son had remained largely unfazed by the strange incident, the landlord himself was deeply disturbed. The experience unsettled him so much that he chose to leave the pub altogether. As for the bones, they were, according to the former barman, reconsecrated and buried.[13]

As for the Grey Man, his identity remains a mystery, and probably always will.

Dead but Awake

7.
THE SECRETS OF THE CELLAR NIGHTCLUB

It was a sad day in 2019 when Tim Hopkins, manager of the Cellar nightclub in central Oxford, locked its doors for the final time. An ongoing dispute with the landlords had made it impossible for him to continue running what had long been one of the city's most beloved live music venues. Over the years, the Cellar had hosted popular acts such as Supergrass, Dawn Penn and The Young Knives along with thousands of long forgotten bands.

The venue itself was unlike any other, tucked beneath the city, with shadowy alcoves surrounding the main stage, which in medieval times was the site of a great fireplace.

The venue was formed from a section of Oxford's underground tunnel network, which once linked several of the university's colleges. In later years, it served as the university's wine cellar, hence the name. It was an atmospheric club, just the sort of place one could imagine being haunted. And as it happens, some people truly believed it was, including a man who we shall call Mr Chief, who in May 2023, recounted to me his brush with the paranormal there, an experience which took place back in the 1980s.

Mr Chief's Account;

> "It was 2 am, there was a lock in at the club, at the bottom end of the bar where you have the alcoves, just going past the walkway, I saw the figure of a woman walk along the walkway and walk straight through the wall, I told my mate working on the bar "f--k me I've just

seen a ghost", he said "don't tell me down here, tell me at the top of the stairs, wait till we are outside."

Outside the barman asked me what I had seen? I told him that I saw the figure of a woman walking through a wall, the bar man said "Oh no, if you talk about her inside the club, the following day you will see that she has wrecked the place", the bar man was right, I worked as a telecoms engineer for the Post office, I would start early and one morning I went to the cellar to fit some cables, I saw first-hand that the chairs and tables were scattered all over the place, everything was trashed.

I asked what had happened and was told that Fred had been around last night, the name people had given the poltergeist, although the consensus was that the resident ghost was female."

Mr Chief told me that the phantasmal woman had walked through a bricked-up wall which leads to numerous cells and alcoves, which would have carried on to other buildings, in years gone by.[14]

I discovered that Frewin Court, the narrow alley that once led to the nightclub, was known as Bridewell Lane from the late sixteenth century until the nineteenth. I was intrigued to learn that in the early seventeenth century, The street was home to the Bridewell workhouse and house of correction, institutions intended to punish the able-bodied destitute who refused to work, often through whipping.

In 1638, the mayor of Oxford complained that inmates held in the barred cellar of the local workhouse were frequently begging from people passing by—and had even been given tools to aid their escape.[15]

Although the cellar nightclub was based in a different building from the Bridewell institution. Chief told me that the arches of the alcoves in the venue, looked like entrances to cells and on the ceiling, you could see where the bars had been cut off, the windows in the back bar also seemed to have sawn off bars.

It's clear then, that The Cellar nightclub was situated in a place with a rather grim and storied past.

I'm fairly certain that over the years, plenty of drunken brawls at The Cellar nightclub ended with a table or two getting flipped. But there seems to have been one room-wrecker the door staff couldn't handle, a ghostly woman who, by all accounts, really doesn't appreciate being talked about in public...

Because if her ears start burning.... the tables start turning.

Oliver Shaw performing at the Tomohawk Xmas party in the Cellar 2002, being watched by a punter who seemingly has no eyes.
{Photograph} Tom McDonnell

Dead but Awake

8.
PEMBROKE COLLEGE: ROOM 136

In May 2018, I had the pleasure of interviewing Jun, a PPE student at Oxford who claimed to have witnessed some very strange occurrences at Pembroke College. I was especially fortunate to speak with him, as he was scheduled to fly home just a few days later, to Georgetown, Utah, USA.

Jun had been through quite an ordeal and was convinced that his lodgings at Pembroke College were haunted. His account was, to say the least, deeply disturbing.

We met at the Oxford Modern Art Café to discuss his experience over coffee and later made our way to Pembroke College. Jun began the interview by admitting he hadn't really believed in ghosts... until his own encounter. It was a promising start; there's always a certain weight to a story when it comes from a former sceptic.

In Jun's own words, here is what unfolded over the course of several unsettling weeks in room 136, staircase 13 of Pembroke college.

> It was the Wednesday of the second week of Michaelmas term, when I awoke in the middle of the night and discovered a figure stood by the curtained windows, it was dark and I initially assumed the curtains were flapping in the breeze, as soon as I realised it seemed to be the figure of a person it disappeared, this vision was over in a matter of seconds.
>
> Being barely awake I put it down to my imagination, it was exactly two weeks later when I next saw the figure, again I had just woken up but this time I could clearly see the

person as moonlight shone through the open curtains: this person or ghost, was wearing a nurses uniform which looked old fashioned, probably early/mid-20th century, she had an ashen face, light blonde hair, and without any discernible facial expression, I could tell her eyes were fixated on me, I remember thinking at the time how her uniform seemed filthy, old and yellowing. As soon as I jumped up from the bed, she disappeared.

Exactly two weeks later, I saw her again, but this time she was not alone, and it was during the day, on this occasion I was very sick from tonsillitis and was taking a nap around 4pm. I heard two people walk into my room, I was very groggy and assumed it was the college nurse and the porter, coming to check on my condition, it then occurred to me, in my half asleep state, that no one was aware of my illness, I hadn't informed anyone, I opened my eyes, and saw the same blonde nurse stood over me, staring at me from the righthand side of the bed, she laid her hand on my chest as if she was going to check my heart beat, I could feel her hand on my chest, as she touched me I felt a strange numb sort of electric shock, I couldn't move, the only thing I could do was look away, when I turned my head to the left, I saw a small, well-dressed man sat on a chair next to the bed, the man was staring at me. He was wearing a smart black suit, perhaps I was delirious, but he seemed to have two small horns sprouting from his forehead, I tried to scream for help, but the tonsillitis had weakened my voice, the man slowly faded into an orange light.

Perhaps I passed out, when I regained consciousness, it was late into the night, I had a dreadful inkling that something strange was about to occur, this feeling was confirmed when I saw what can only be described as an avalanche of long, blonde hair descending the wall from the ceiling right above my head. I was paralysed with fear, I closed my eyes and hoped it was all just a dream, when I reopened my eyes, it was morning.

The first two visitations were interesting, but the third time really frightened me, I had to tell some friends, thankfully they were sympathetic, You're the sixth person I've shared this with.

I asked the domestic manager if I could change rooms. Instead of mentioning ghosts, I said the floor was uncomfortable to walk on, that it felt uneven, the domestic manager explained that it was an old building {what did I expect?} but said she would add my name to the room transfer list. She must've thought it was a weird request, especially with less than two weeks left in my nine-month study period.

I decided to visit the nearby Catholic church of Holyrood on the Abingdon Road, I asked the priest if he could spare some holy water, naturally my request came as a surprise and he laughed when I told him about the ghosts, he kindly obliged when he realised I was completely serious.

I sprinkled holy water around my room, and thankfully, the phantoms did not return. That said, their visitations had followed a pattern...every other Wednesday, If the pattern holds, I'll be long gone before their next appearance".[16]

I was absolutely fascinated by Jun's account and began to wonder if his accommodation had ever been used as a hospital, perhaps during wartime. Interestingly, Pembroke's college archivist informed Jun of a rumour that the site of his living quarters had been used as a military hospital in the first world war, naturally I decided to investigate.

Jun's room is in the relatively modern North Quad of the college, which was added during an expansion in 1962, Before the expansion, the buildings were private properties on Beef Lane and Pembroke Street. Acquired gradually by Pembroke over many years, these properties were eventually transformed into staircases 12 to 18 of the North Quad.

All the properties on Beef Lane were eventually fully incorporated into the college and gated off, making them private and no longer accessible to the public. The buildings on Pembroke Street—most of which are Grade II listed—have also been reconfigured: what were once their front doors now serve as back entrances.

A friend of mine, Nina, lived on Staircase 11, she informed me that most of these buildings are Jacobean and had traditionally housed Oxford's Jewish population, both before and after the expulsion of the Jews from England. [17]

I wondered if the later-incorporated buildings had ever served a military purpose. Oxford played a significant role in providing hospital care during the Great War; many college buildings were part of the 3rd Southern General Hospital, one of the largest military hospitals in the Southeast.

When the Radcliffe Infirmary struggled to cope with the influx of soldiers suffering from malaria, the neighbouring college, Somerville, stepped in to provide much-needed assistance. Just three months into the war, around 250,000 Belgian and Serbian refugees had arrived in England, many bearing severe injuries and psychological trauma. In response, the Town Hall and the Oxford Examination Schools were converted into makeshift hospitals. Serbian refugees were housed at Queen's College, while Belgians found shelter at Ruskin College.

I discovered that Pembroke was requisitioned by the military in 1915; however, instead of being converted into a military hospital, its rooms were occupied by flight instructors training at the nearby School of Military Aeronautics, so, it seems as that our spectral nurse was

Jun looking up to his haunted room.
{Photograph} Tom McDonnell

unlikely to have been connected to the military. [18]

Staircase 13, where Jun lived, is located precisely where 23 and 24 Pembroke Street once stood, 24-27 Pembroke Street were the last houses to be purchased by Pembroke, prior to the 1960s, these buildings were owned by Christchurch College, 26 and 27 Pembroke Street were deemed unfit for habitation and were subsequently demolished. However, the current student accommodation on Staircase 13 integrated the original 16th-century buildings that remained.

I spent a great deal of time researching the former occupants of 23 and 24 Pembroke Street and uncovered a curious mix of bespoke tradesmen and women, many with occupations that evoke a long-forgotten past. For example, in the mid-1800s, Number 23 was home to William J. Hill, a glazier, and C. Gooden, a bookbinder. In 1852, a Miss S. Rogers lived at Number 24, earning her living by making straw hats, surely a booming business in Victorian Oxford.

Several college servants employed by Christ Church also resided at Number 24, which is hardly surprising given that the property was owned by the college. Christ Church, however, was perhaps not the most generous of employers. Historical records reveal that two of their college servants living at Number 24 were convicted of game-related crimes. George Leach was found guilty of trespassing while hunting rabbits in 1861, and another servant, George Burrill, was convicted of shooting game with a gun in 1838. It is Burrill, in fact, who has piqued my interest in relation to the haunting of Jun's room.

Although I found no evidence of foul play at either 23 or 24, I did discover that on 12 February 1852, Eliza Burrill—the eldest daughter of George Burrill—passed away at the house at just seventeen years old. [19]

I decided to discuss the spectres of Pembroke College

with local historian Marilyn Yurdan. When I brought up the mystery of the phantom nurse, Marilyn explained that in Victorian times, resident nurses—often employed to care for children—wore uniforms that closely resembled those of hospital nurses. Their attire was also similar to that worn by housemaids and female college servants of the era.

Upon hearing this, it occurred to me that the phantom nurse might not have been a hospital nurse at all, but rather a private nurse called in to care for a sick child, in this case Eliza Burrill. I also began to wonder if the man in black was the apparition of George Burrill himself, dressed in his smart black work uniform, keeping a bedside vigil for his dying daughter.

I discussed this theory with Jun, who agreed that I had uncovered some credible possibilities. He felt, however, that during the third sighting, the man in black struck him as a rather sinister presence. Still, he conceded that the man's grim demeanour might have simply reflected the gravity of the situation, that of a father helplessly watching his ailing daughter slip away on her deathbed.

Perhaps we will never quite crack the mystery of the Pembroke college spectres, their identities forever obscured in the fog of time, nevertheless, I believe my detective work has uncovered some plausible candidates.

Although Jun told me he had never been a firm believer in ghosts, I felt compelled to ask whether he could recall any past experiences that might have been supernatural in nature. Some individuals seem to possess a certain magnetic pull for paranormal energies; an ability not necessarily rooted in a desire to attract such forces.

Jun leaned back and gave the question some thought, a question which seemed to trigger a flashback to an event from his childhood. It was an event he could barely recall, he explained, but one his mother would never forget.

Dead but Awake

As a toddler, Jun lived in an apartment in South Korea with his mother, his father was working abroad at the time.

One day, there was a knock at the apartment door. When Jun's mother opened it, she was met by a strange, middle-aged woman who asked for a glass of water, what puzzled her the most was how the woman had managed to reach the apartment at all, it was a gated community, and

Jun, outside staircase 13
{Photograph} Tom McDonnell

access required a key to enter the compound.

After drinking the water, the strange woman's demeanour changed dramatically. She began shouting aggressively at Jun's mother, claiming that her ancestors were furious with her and her family and that the only way to appease them was to join a particular religious cult. But Jun's mother is no fool. She quickly realised that the woman's behaviour was probably part of a scam, one that's apparently quite common in South Korea, a scheme designed to con superstitious folk out of their money. The woman was promptly and firmly shown the door.

However, just a few days later, young Jun began to exhibit an unsettling habit, he would stare, as though transfixed, at one of the apartment walls, then suddenly burst into tears. Understandably, his mother grew concerned by this abrupt change in his behaviour. She couldn't help but wonder if it was somehow linked to the strange woman's visit, perhaps even fearing that a curse had been placed on her son, after giving this frightening situation some serious thought, she decided that the best option might be to remedy her son's condition by spiritual means, she invited a Buddhist Monk to perform an exorcism, an ancient ritual which thankfully seemed to work, Jun reverted back to his usual happy go lucky self.

It occurred to me that this early experience, during Jun's formative years, may have subconsciously inspired him to carry out his own makeshift exorcism nearly two decades later in Room 136.

As an aside, I noted that Jun lives in Georgetown, not far from the location where *The Exorcist* was filmed. I couldn't help but imagine that a film based on Jun's own supernatural experiences might offer audiences a similarly chilling experience.[20]

Dead but Awake

9.
WHAT BECOMES OF THE BROKEN HEARTED

The building that houses the Old Bank Hotel at 94 High Street was, as one might expect, once home to a bank, operating in that capacity from 1775 until 1998. That's when local art dealer Jeremy Mogford purchased the property and transformed it into the plush hotel it is today, Magpie Lane runs alongside the hotel, and along this narrow stretch, a series of wooden beams are visible on the hotel's exterior. If you glance up, about seven meters from the High Street, you'll spot a beam with a date inscribed: 1588, a pivotal year in British history, marking England's victory over the Spanish Armada.

There is a falsehood, often repeated by tour guides, that the wooden beam was crafted from timber salvaged from the Armada. It's a nice story, but I've never seen any evidence to support it.

The date carved into the timber does inform us that the house was built in 1588, not a particularly important house at the time, it is presently occupied by The Quad restaurant, the dining area of the Old Bank Hotel.

In the 16th century, Magpie Lane was infamous as the place to secure the services of prostitutes. Originally known as 'Grope Cxxt Lane', it was later changed to Grove Lane. The lane's current name was inspired by a tavern with a pub sign featuring a magpie.

Both the Old Bank Hotel and Magpie Lane are said to be haunted by the same tragic spectre, Prudence Burcote.

In 1642, as the English Civil War escalated, King Charles I made Oxford his base for the next four years, with the city enduring constant siege.

The King resided in Oxford's largest college, Christ

Church, while his wife, Henrietta Maria, stayed nearby in the lavish buildings of Merton College. A secret tunnel once connected the two colleges, and small traces of it can still be seen today in the gardens of Corpus Christi, a college nestled between Christ Church and Merton.

Queen Henrietta Maria arrived with a small army, all of whom, like her, were French and Catholic, they marched along Merton Street and Magpie Lane, protecting their Queen.

At the time, the Old Bank Hotel was a townhouse occupied by the Puritan Burcote family, who, like many townspeople, secretly supported Parliament. They resented the king and the turmoil his presence brought to the city. Initially, King Charles I tried to appear friendly to the locals, but the longer he was trapped in Oxford, the more his demeanour soured. He was eventually driven to madness by paranoia, and ordered the arrest and execution of random locals, hoping to instil fear in the people of Oxford and ensure they would never dare assist the enemy.

The Burcotes not only harboured a deep resentment for the King but also for Catholics. As Puritans, they rejected the concepts of sainthood and purgatory, and they opposed any church with a hierarchical structure, such as a church with bishops and popes.

The Burcotes had a seventeen-year-old daughter, Prudence, who often caught the eye of one of the French soldiers marching past her home daily. One could easily imagine a romantic scene unfolding, young Prudence peering out of her bedroom window, meeting the gaze of a handsome French soldier who, perhaps feeling homesick and lonely, found himself drawn to her.

A romance blossomed between the Puritan maid and the soldier, much to the disapproval of both Prudence's family and the French contingent. Alas, as with many tales of star-crossed lovers, fate would not allow for a happy ending. The French lover mysteriously disappeared in early 1643, just a few months into their affair.

The fate of the soldier remains a mystery. His sudden disappearance from Oxford wasn't particularly unusual-it was a time of war, and troops were frequently redeployed across the southeast, often with little warning. But he disappeared without saying farewell to Prudence, there were no letters, no contact whatsoever. Poor Prudence was devastated, completely heartbroken, if anyone knocked on the front door, she would answer in the hope that her lover had returned, she often walked the lanes searching for him, after a few months of this hopeless despair, the inconsolable girl was resigned to the fact she would never see him again, this all-consuming grief took its toll, Prudence stayed in her room and starved herself to death, and that was the end of her… or was it?

Over the years, hotel guests have occasionally reported seeing a short, young girl in a brown dress and white peaked cap—commonly believed to be Prudence, also known as the Brown Lady of Magpie Lane. She is said to be a particular kind of ghost: a poltergeist. Guests have described trying to read in their rooms, only for the lights to dim on their own, and kitchen staff have reported finding cutlery and utensils mysteriously displaced.

In 2015, I spoke with an elderly lady named Barbara, who had worked at the Barclays bank that once occupied the building before its current incarnation, without mentioning the buildings alleged haunted history, I asked if she had noticed any strange happenings when she worked there as a bank clerk, she told me that in two rooms on the first floor {above what is now the Quad restaurant's kitchen} the temperature would sometimes inexplicably drop, regardless of the time of year, these rooms persistently had electrical issues, light bulbs would flicker on and off, occasionally the radio would switch

Magpie Lane
By Gus Mills

itself on, Barbara was not surprised in the slightest when I mentioned the legend of the Old Banks poltergeist.[21]

Another source confided that staff working late into the night often heard unexplained footsteps echoing from the upstairs rooms, yet no one was ever found. It's said the legend of Prudence Burcote was not taken lightly by those who worked there.

My friend Marilyn knew someone at the bank who also claimed to have heard phantom footsteps in the room above—but this time accompanied by the faint shuffle of a dress brushing across the floor.[22]

On 2 September 2023, Darryl, a former bank employee, told me that he was one of several staff members who had actually seen Prudence. He described the familiar pattern of events that typically preceded her appearance, which often took place in the basement where the safes were kept.

"The room would always go cold, the hairs on the back of your neck would stand up on end and then you would see her, fleetingly"[23]

In the early 1990s, a friend of mine, Eva Wagner, used to lead ghost tours around Oxford. On one occasion, the manager of the bank happened to join her tour. When Eva shared the story of Prudence, the manager interrupted and said, "Oh, I know Prudence. She would upset everything. She'd sit in the very chair a guest was about to take. But what really drove the staff mad was when the office girls were carrying huge stacks of files—Prudence would tug at their elbows, and all the files would go crashing to the floor."

Eva also discovered that in the 1920s, before the building became a bank, it served as the residence of the warden of University College. On one occasion, the warden hosted an American professor and his wife for tea. They were invited upstairs to the sitting room, where they waited with the warden's wife. When the tea failed to arrive on time, she excused herself, saying, "I'm just going to the kitchen to see what's going on."

When the warden's wife returned, the guests had smiles on their faces and said "It's very charming, that you dress your maid up in puritan clothes"

She replied "No our maid is a flapper {it was the 1920's} and she's still in the kitchen, what you've seen is our ghost Prudence, and she doesn't like strangers" [24]

The warden's wife's response certainly wiped the smiles from the guests faces.

There have also been reports of Prudence appearing on Magpie Lane, a strange phenomenon I've personally witnessed no fewer than thirty-nine times. On occasion, the streetlights along the lane mysteriously flicker out, only to come back on moments later. According to tradition, this is the work of Prudence: the lights dim as she passes beneath them, pacing up and down the lane in eternal search of her lost lover—a lover who will never return.

10.
THE GHOSTS OF WADHAM COLLEGE

Wadham College is one of my favourite places to visit in Oxford. It is said to be the last building in England constructed by a Master Mason—someone who served as both architect and builder. The college's foundation also comes with an intriguing backstory.

Nicholas Wadham, a gentleman from Devonshire, was a wealthy landowner who, upon his death in 1609, left a substantial fortune to fund the establishment of an Oxford college. The responsibility for fulfilling his wish fell to his wife, Dorothy, who acted swiftly, but it was by no means a simple task.

She faced stiff competition for a prime piece of land located on the site of the old Austin Friary, Fortunately, the Wadhams had influential allies. King James I himself wrote a letter of support to Oxford's local government on Dorothy's behalf, and his royal endorsement ensured she was given priority over rival bidders.

Still, Dorothy's battles weren't just external. She also had to deal with a few less-than-thrilled family members, disgruntled over what they considered meagre inheritances from Nicholas's estate. Starting a college, it seems, requires not just vision and wealth, but also a thick skin and a royal connection or two.

Dorothy threw herself into the task with remarkable determination. She personally hired every workman involved in the project, and within just four years of her husband's death, Wadham College was not only built but fully operational. No detail escaped her attention—she appointed each member of staff herself, from the very first warden and fellows to, quite charmingly, the college cook.

Though she poured her heart and soul into realising her husband's vision, Dorothy never actually set foot in the college she brought to life. By the time she undertook this formidable task, she was already in her mid-seventies—and in the 17th century, a journey from Devon to Oxford was no small feat. One imagines she preferred to oversee matters from the comfort of her drawing room, rather than endure the bone-rattling ordeal of a long and arduous ride in a horse and carriage.

It is truly remarkable to think that Dorothy orchestrated every step of Wadham College's creation through letter correspondence alone. But what she likely never suspected, indeed, what would have been beyond the imagination of even a woman as capable as Dorothy, is that the college she so diligently built would one day be said to house residents she not only outlived, but who had walked its grounds many moons before the first foundation stones were laid.

Seventy years before the construction of Wadham College, Henry VIII launched the dissolution of the monasteries, a sweeping and revolutionary policy that led to the disbanding of friaries, nunneries, and monasteries across England, Wales, and Ireland. The Crown seized their income, sold off their assets, and repurposed or destroyed centuries-old institutions of faith. The entire operation was orchestrated under the watchful eye of Thomas Cromwell, Henry's chief minister and architect of religious reform.

Naturally, the dissolution sparked outrage among the nation's monastic communities. Yet, just before the suppression of the Austin Friary in Oxford, the site was inspected by Doctor John London, acting on behalf of Thomas Cromwell. Interestingly, the doctor seemed to believe that the dissolution might, in fact, be in the best interests of the Austin Friars themselves, his report stated, "If they do not forsake their houses, their houses will forsake them", The Austin Friary was in a state of ruin, and the friars who were ultimately evicted had been living in conditions of abject poverty.[25]

However, it seems that at least one of the friars never actually left, perhaps bound to the place by forces not so easily dissolved.

A cluster of ghostly sightings were reported during the 1960s. On the night of 28 December 1968, Mr. Arthur Rees, the head porter, was working the night shift. As he returned from the Rear Quadrangle and passed through the archway of Staircase 4, he suddenly heard a strange voice telling him to 'look to the right.' He did so—and there, illuminated by moonlight, was a robed, hooded monk lurching around the outside of the college chapel. When Mr. Rees shone his torch at the figure, the light passed straight through it.

The hooded spectre then floated silently along the college wall and drifted into the dining hall, vanishing at the stairway. The entire encounter lasted approximately five minutes. An extensive search of the buildings followed—but no trace of the monk was found, it was certainly a night patrol that would not be easily forgotten.

One might be tempted to assume the night porter had indulged in a little too much port over the Christmas period. However, Oxford college porters—many of whom are retired police officers—tend to take their duties very seriously. Responsible for the safety of hundreds of students, they are not the type to drink on the job or casually claim to have seen a ghost without good reason.

John Richardson, a collector of ghost stories, heard the account firsthand from Arthur Rees himself, whom he described as generally "sceptical of the supernatural" [26]

In June 1967, no fewer than four college scouts witnessed an apparition while cleaning the dining hall after dinner. The sighting occurred at around 11:30 p.m. One of the scouts, a Mr. C.S., later gave the following account of the incident.

"It was about six feet tall and looked like a priest, it was definitely a human figure, after a few seconds, the figure vanished, and I was staring into an empty hall. I heard footsteps and beat it quickly out of the hall".

It is worth noting that Mr. C.S. had worked as a scout at the college for nine years and had never heard any mention of ghosts haunting Wadham before.

It would be entirely understandable if the college scouts were feeling a bit jittery at the time, on 20 May, just a few weeks before the manifestation, a disturbing incident occurred at Wadham College. Geoffrey Johnston Holt, a third-year chemistry student, attempted to murder a fellow Wadhamite, Norman James Port. Holt had left a beaker of water laced with sodium cyanide next to the wash basin in Port's room, hoping he would unknowingly drink the poison.

What made the act even more unsettling was the apparent lack of motive. Though Holt and Port had crossed paths at a few Christian Union meetings, they barely knew each other, and Holt reportedly held no grudge, fortunately Holt confessed to a friend what he had done and the police intervened before anything terrible happened, Holt was put on trial for attempted murder, he also faced an additional charge of stealing cyanide from Oxford University, he was spared jail but spent eighteen months in a psychiatric hospital, he later moved to Birmingham where he taught religious studies, One can only imagine the relief of his students that he'd left chemistry behind.[27]

Clearly, Wadham was a rather peculiar place in the 1960s. Around this time, Maurice Howes, head steward with twenty years of service, claimed he frequently heard

Wadham College
By Gus Mills

phantom footsteps above his office, which was based directly beneath the dining hall, Howes said "The footsteps have walked down the Hall, but I've never heard them going back. Many times, I've dashed up there only to find the Hall deserted, I've never seen the ghost".

The head chef confirmed the head steward's account, adding that he had also heard phantom footsteps echoing through the dining Hall on several occasions.[28]

Over the years at Wadham, there have been numerous accounts of a mysterious ghost known only as the Wadham Knocker. On many nights, Mr. Arthur Rees and other porters reported hearing loud knocking and prolonged kicking on the college's large wooden gates, as if someone were urgently trying to get in or desperately sought attention. Despite extensive searches of the grounds—and even along Parks Road—no one has ever laid eyes on the elusive Knocker. Security cameras, too, have failed to capture any trace of the entity. I couldn't help but wonder whether it might be the spirit of a displaced monk, still longing to return to the land he was cast out from nearly six centuries ago.

A chance encounter with two American summer school students led me to believe that the Wadham Knocker might also be active within the college itself, each summer, around 3,000 international students come to Oxford to attend short study courses. Among the most popular subjects are International Law, English Literature, and Shakespeare Studies. The summer students get to immerse themselves in the full Oxford experience, including the rare opportunity to live within the college itself.

On 14 July 2019, I met two students, Taylor and Kayla, who were attending a summer course at Wadham. During our conversation, I happened to mention *Dead but Awake*, which immediately caught their attention. They became animated and curious, eager to hear about any ghost stories connected to Wadham. When I mentioned the legend of the Wadham Knocker, they began recounting several strange experiences they had personally witnessed.

Taylor and Kayla shared room three on stairwell five, they both claimed to have heard someone knocking on their door, only to discover there was no one on the other side, the students also claimed to have witnessed doors inexplicably open by themselves, and on several occasions, both had seen a motion activated light come on in the bathroom, despite there being no visible presence inside.

The most unsettling of these incidents happened to Kayla. One afternoon, she was suddenly overcome with fatigue and decided to lie down for a nap, but as she lay in her bed, chills began to run up and down her spine, she described what followed as "absolutely terrifying", she claimed that she felt the distinct sensation of someone actually sitting down on her legs, when Kayla opened her eyes, she realised that there was no other visible presence in the room, any thoughts of fatigue escaped her mind as she sprinted straight out of the room.[29]

I found this incident particularly intriguing, as it echoed reports from the 1960s involving staff at the porters' lodge. Several described a strange sensation of being pressed down upon from above—so intensely that it became difficult to breathe. Some porters who had taken a nap also reported feeling an invisible, oppressive force bearing down on them with such weight that they were unable to rise from their beds. [30]

I later realised that Stairwell 5, where Taylor and Kayla had been staying, is close to where Mr. A.R. witnessed the apparition vanish in 1968.

Wadham is a college that I believe warrants further investigation—a quaint, picturesque sandstone building that seems to harbour some remarkably loud and restless spirits.

Dead but Awake

11.
THE LINTON ROAD POLTERGEISTS

Linton Road is an attractive residential street in leafy North Oxford, most of the people who live in the area are academics or students, it also appears to accommodate several poltergeists.

In late 2023, a young lady told me about some strange happenings that had taken place in her family home on Linton Road, an old manor house which she felt was occupied by two distinct presences, here is her account.

"One presence is warm and welcoming, you can hear this invisible person walking through the hallways and opening doors, my family believe it's the spirit of the housekeeper of the people we bought the house from, very occasionally she will really make her presence known, one day, when I was much younger, I was having a conversation with my mother, worried about making changes in my life when suddenly a book flew off the bookshelf, it was a book written by Erich Fromm, *Fear of freedom*, it certainly felt like the spirit was sending me a message.

"There's another part of the house however, near to what was originally the main front door, not used these days, there is a dark energy in that part of the house, which is a section of the building that is seldom used".[31]

The woman's account is certainly fascinating, but it turns out that paranormal activity has also been reported just across the road from the Manor House, I recently discovered that Wolfson College student accommodation occupies the site of a former nursing home, where a particularly strange event is reportedly said to have taken place.

On 21 August 2023, a former Wolfson student named Gary O'Brien shared a peculiar story with me. While living in the college lodgings on Linton Road, Gary once found himself frantically searching for his front door key. After turning his room upside down, he eventually opened a drawer and discovered a small box. Inside, perfectly balanced on a ring, was his missing key. To this day, he has no idea how it got there or how it ended up so precisely placed.

Given that a nursing home once occupied the site, it's safe to assume that many people passed away in that area. As for the identity of the mischievous spirit who decided to toy with Gary's keys, well, that will likely remain a mystery.[32]

12.
FEAR AND MISCHIEF AT THE MITRE INN

As of early 2024, an Italian chain restaurant now occupies the site of The Mitre, a former 14th-century coaching inn on the high street. Much to the dismay of traditionalists and real ale enthusiasts, Lincoln College granted the lease to the restaurant not long after the COVID-19 pandemic.

The building is, however, said to be haunted by not one, but two ghosts. Personally, I'd raise a glass if they managed to scare the current occupiers out and the place reverted to being a traditional pub. As one disgruntled tour guide put it: "Visitors don't come to Oxford to visit Italian restaurants".[33]

That said, I wouldn't have envied the job of landlord—or landlady—at the Mitre in the 17th century. It was no easy task, as poor Mrs. Eunice Lazenby discovered in the small hours of 21 December 1682.

The previous evening, three members of All Souls College had been out celebrating the re-opening of the Mermaid Tavern on Broad Street, which had just resumed business after a three-month closure. (And in case you're wondering what became of the Mermaid—it wasn't swallowed by a chain restaurant. It was renamed the White Horse in the 1830s and still stands today, right next to Blackwell's Bookshop.)

By midnight, the three revellers had grown hungry and made their way to the Mitre, where a young boy admitted them. They asked for food, but the boy explained that everyone was asleep. "Where does Mrs. Lazenby sleep?" they demanded. The boy, perhaps too helpfully, pointed to a ground-floor window.

Drunk and impatient, the men began hammering on

the glass and shouting for meat. Eunice called back that it was far too late and she had no intention of getting out of bed. Their response was a torrent of abuse: "Popish whore," "old Popish bitch," and even that she deserved to have her throat cut. Terrified, Eunice collapsed into a fit. Three hours later, she was found dead—frightened, quite literally, to death.[34]

The three All Souls men were compelled by the authorities to pen a letter of apology to Eunice's husband—a pitiful reparation for the terror and grief they had wrought. Perhaps it is for this reason that Mrs. Lazenby is said to drift along the second floor of the Mitre, shrouded in sombre grey. One can only hope she does not linger in eternal fear… but rather, that she is now the one to be feared.

The Mitre's other ghost is said to be that of a monk. He likely never crosses paths with Eunice, as he is believed to haunt the old tunnels beneath the building—passageways supposedly built during the Reformation to provide Catholics with an escape route in case Henry VIII's agents arrived to break up secret masses.

The story goes that in the 17th century, the landlord and landlady of the Mitre were devout Catholics, though they had to keep their faith hidden in what were staunchly Protestant times. They would sometimes host a visiting monk who came to say Mass in secret, and in times of danger, he could be concealed within the building.

One day, as the monk conducted Mass in the cellar, a loud knock came at the door, it was the authorities. In a panic, the monk fled into a hidden passage: a tunnel which ran beneath the high street, connecting the Mitre to the Chequers pub directly opposite. The tunnel emerged into what is now known as the Monk's Bar in the Chequers. Heavy furniture was quickly piled against the entrance of the passage to hide his escape.

The Monk's Bar and the Grandfather Clock at the Chequers—a pub where, according to a barmaid in September 2025, glasses have been known to mysteriously fly off the shelves.
(Photograph) Tom McDonnell

Unfortunately, the landlord and landlady were arrested and taken to prison, leaving no one behind who knew the monk was hiding in the tunnel. The other end of the passage was also sealed off, as both pubs were now under guard. Trapped and alone, the monk called out and clawed at the blockages in vain, until eventually, he suffocated in the darkness.

In more recent times, patrons sitting in the bar at the Mitre have reported hearing strange scratching sounds coming from the floorboards. Tour guide Nuala Young once told me that, in years past, she could lead visitors down into the cellar to see the entrance to the hidden passage. But, as she put it, "health and safety has done away with all that."

These days, the soft hum of restaurant muzak tends to drown out any eerie scratching noises—but if you listen closely, you might still catch the faint scraping of the monk's bleeding fingernails as he desperately tries to escape his claustrophobic tomb. The Chequers pub, directly opposite, lays claim to a haunting of its own. Scratching sounds are often heard behind the fireplace—right where the tunnel from the Mitre is said to have once emerged. According to tradition, the ghostly monk is sometimes seen when the old grandfather clock is wound up, a spectral reminder of a soul who never found his way out...[35]

Nuala also mentioned that numerous tunnels have been discovered beneath the High Street in more recent times, often uncovered during modern drainage works. Of all these hidden passageways, the tunnel connecting the Mitre to the Chequers is one of the few that remains intact.

13.
THE RUINS OF GODSTOW

For a time, I lived in the charming village of Wolvercote in north Oxford, surrounded by fantastic pubs like The White Hart, The Plough and The Trout Inn. Just a two-minute stroll from my home lay Port Meadow— 'Oxford's oldest monument'—a vast stretch of common land covering 400 acres, its landscape largely unchanged since prehistoric times. It was here that Bronze Age inhabitants of Oxford buried their dead. Thankfully, the meadow has been protected from development since the tenth century, when King Alfred granted the freemen of Oxford the right to graze livestock on the land—a right recorded in the Domesday Book of 1086, and one that is still exercised by the freemen to this day.

C.S. Lewis and J.R.R. Tolkien often strolled through Port Meadow, deep in conversation about books, ideas, and faith as they made their way from one cosy pub to another. One of their favourite haunts was The Trout Inn, which overlooks the Thames. Just a two-minute stroll from the pub, beside the banks of Trout Island, lie the imposing ruins of Godstow Nunnery, a haunting place well worth exploring. A place which is forever linked to a doomed love affair: the infamous dalliance of King Henry II.

The complexities of King Henry II's love life played an unlikely role in the creation of Oxford University. In the 1160s, England found itself in a cold war with France, fuelled partly by religious tensions, but further strained by Henry's politically charged marriage to his third cousin, Eleanor of Aquitaine, a former queen of France who had divorced Louis VII in 1152. In 1167, amid rising hostilities, Henry II banned English students from studying in France. Until then, it had been common for

The Ruins of Godstow
{Photograph} Tom McDonnell

English scholars to attend the Sorbonne in Paris.

The travel ban became a catalyst for English students to gravitate toward Oxford, which was already emerging as a centre of learning. Wandering scholars and monks, who preached the word of God and debated scripture, had begun to settle in the city. Over time, various monastic orders, including the Benedictines, Augustinians, and later the Dominicans and Franciscans established a presence there. Oxford's growing reputation for ecclesiastical education spread across Europe, reaching as far as Italy. In the early 13th century, Francis of Assisi himself is said to have sent Franciscan friars to Oxford to establish a community and contribute to its academic and spiritual life

Although Oxford University did not admit women until the late 19th century, Medieval Oxford was home to institutions where women could receive an education, often under the guidance of nuns and focused on the study of Holy Scripture. One such place was Godstow Nunnery, founded in 1133.

Legend has it that Rosamond Clifford, a woman renowned for her beauty, was educated at Godstow Nunnery. She captured the heart of King Henry II, who—despite being on the brink of war with France in 1166, still found time to further complicate his life by falling deeply in love with her. By 1173, their affair had become serious, and Rosamond is believed to have borne him two sons. Though Henry had many mistresses, he treated Rosamond differently, flaunting their relationship openly—an act that greatly angered his wife, Queen Eleanor.

However, the king's relationship with his wife and family was deeply dysfunctional. It was likely no coincidence that his affair with Rosamond became more public in 1173—the very year he placed Queen Eleanor under house arrest for supporting their sons' revolt against him. Eleanor would go on to spend the next sixteen years confined in various locations across England.[36]

This is where the story takes a truly fantastical turn. So protective was the king of Rosamond that he arranged for her to be hidden away in a secret location—a secluded garden guarded by a labyrinth near his hunting palace at Woodstock. The entrance to the maze was watched over by one of the king's most trusted aides, Sir Thomas, who held the end of a silver thread that wound its way through the labyrinth and led directly to Rosamond.

Eleanor was consumed with jealousy—furious that a woman half her age had captured her husband's heart. In 1176, while the King was in France, she decided something had to be done—something drastic. Though technically under house arrest, her confinement was relatively lenient. She was permitted to attend special occasions, such as Christmas, as the King's primary concern was preventing her from communicating with their sons. In hindsight, he may well have wished her confinement had been more strictly enforced.

According to legend, Eleanor arrived at Woodstock with a small entourage. Sir Thomas was the first to be killed. Eleanor then personally followed the silver thread through the labyrinth to confront her rival. Upon finding Rosamond, she is said to have offered her a grim choice: drink from a poisoned chalice or be stabbed with a dagger. Rosamond reportedly chose the chalice. However, other, darker versions of the tale claim that she was first roasted between two fires, then forced into a bathtub, where an elderly woman—an acquaintance of Eleanor—slashed both of her arms, leaving her to bleed to death.[37]

According to the Victorian story collector Fred Thacker, another legend has been passed down through the centuries, one that suggests Rosamond met a supernatural end. Thacker noted that as recently as 1870, 'the gypsies of Oxfordshire would say that Rosamond was changed into a Holy Briar, which bled if a twig was plucked".[38]

Regardless of the true circumstances surrounding her death, we can only imagine the king's profound grief upon receiving the news. It is said that he had been considering divorcing Eleanor to marry Rosamond, who was reputed to be the great love of his life. In her honour, he commissioned an elaborate tomb at Godstow, where she was buried. However, two years after the king's death in 1191, the Bishop of Lincoln ordered her body to be removed from the church, declaring her a 'harlot.' She was reburied outside the church grounds. Her second grave, too, did not escape desecration—it was vandalised during the Dissolution of the Monasteries in the 1530s.[39]

Centuries after Rosamond's death, her legend continued to inspire artists; in 1592, poet Samuel Daniel was moved to write *The Complaint of Rosamond*[40], between

1707 and 1837, her tragic tale inspired no fewer than five operas, among them a German composition from 1780 by Anton Schweitzer[41] and an 1834 work by Italian composer Gaetano Donizetti, which has experienced a revival in recent years.[42]

The character of Rosamond has been depicted in at least sixteen novels, Clara Dupont-Monod's 2018 epic historical tome *The Revolt* is the portal for Rosamond's latest literary manifestation.[43]

In the heart of Wolvercote village, there is a street named Rosamund Road, another tribute to a local legend that dates back over nine hundred years. Beyond operas, novels, and street signs, there is said to be one final reminder of Rosamond's presence: and that is Rosamond herself, whose apparition is said to the wander the site of her grave at Godstow.

But Rosamond may not be the only spectre said to haunt the ruins of Godstow Nunnery. According to legend, at dawn on the first of May each year, strange celestial singing can be heard drifting through the crumbling remains of this once-glorious foundation. However, I believe that I have solved the mystery of this ghostly chorus. At that very hour, as part of Oxford's ancient May Day tradition, the choir of Magdalen College School sings from the top of Magdalen College Tower, ushering in the summer with Latin hymns. It is entirely possible that the morning winds carry their voices across the open expanse of Port Meadow, giving rise to the illusion of a spectral choir among the ruins.

Although local legend places Rosamond's ghost among the ruins of Godstow, her presence has also been felt across the river at the nearby Trout Inn, an old pub that may well be the most haunted in Oxford. As a casual and well-loved drinking spot, it seems only fitting that the bar staff have affectionately shortened her name to 'Rosie'.

Dead but Awake

14.
THE SPECTRES OF THE TROUT INN

The Trout Inn, a contender for being Oxfords most haunted pub.
{Photograph} Tom McDonnell

Over the years, The Trout Inn in the village of Wolvercote has been a popular riverside retreat for many Oxford-based authors. With its idyllic setting, it's the perfect spot to enjoy a pint, relax by the water, and watch the resident peacocks as they cheekily attempt to steal your crisps.

Having lived in Wolvercote myself, I often heard stories from both customers and staff at The Trout Inn about sightings of a shadowy figure drifting in and out of view—

usually preceded by a sudden chill in the air.

In 2022, I had the good fortune to meet Heather Sillence, an Australian who had once worked at the pub and encountered all sorts of strange paranormal activity. She has kindly shared her experiences with me.

One of Heathers accounts includes a variation of Rosamond's tragic end. And I guess such variations are hardly surprising, given the ancient roots of Rosamond's legend. This is Heather's account;

> "I live in Sydney, Australia and was studying a Bachelor of Business at the Hotel School Sydney through Southern Cross University. There was a significant period of the degree whereby you had to undertake a paid internship in a hospitality organisation whilst completing various assignments etc.
>
> I had always wanted to go and live for a while in the UK after visiting with my father in my early teenage years and being brought up by my parents on a healthy schedule of British comedy and the BBC.
>
> I think most Australians feel a particular sense of connection to the UK not only because of the Commonwealth formality but also for ancestral bloodlines in many cases. My father is an organist with a love for cathedrals (with many a ghost story!), and my mother an academic and businesswoman (a Vet actually) so my sense of history of the UK was always extremely diverse.
>
> So, taking the opportunity in full, I moved to the UK and chose Oxford for its incredible history, countryside and general demographic and arrived at The Trout in Oxford in October 2013.

The Trout is widely known for its appearances in tv series such as Inspector Morse and Lewis to name a few. It is also said to have been a regular haunt of CS Lewis, Lewis Carroll, Oscar Wilde and J.R.R.Tolkien to sit and write by the river. Really anyone that attended Oxford university is aware of The Trout.

I moved into the top floor, the window you can see above the main entrance, and was regularly awoken at 4am by Krug the peacock who is still around today! For anyone visiting, he particularly enjoys a rump steak and crumbled butter cookies.

The Trout is split into multiple sections based on when newer parts of the building were added on, and the different rooms are named by their respective table numbers. To demonstrate, the newest part of the building (down where the bathrooms are, to the left if facing the front entrance) is called '1-9', then moving along the building you go through the 'bar tables', the room directly opposite the front entrance is the '30s', to the right of the cellar is the '40's' and then the oldest room down to the right is the '50s'.

The 40s and 50s are clearly the oldest parts due to the flooring which is particularly sunken in places and requires you to bend down so as not to bump your head between rooms.

It is clear to see that the 50s did originally have two stories where the roof/floor of the second level was later removed. It is said that this part of the building is from the 1200's and was an Inn for the King and his entourage between trips to the countryside. It is said that his shoes were also made here, and he would visit quite regularly. I can't however tell you which King this was or which century, but it is where our Rosie story starts.

If you've ever walked around The Trout, you may have crossed the bridge on the weir on Godstow Road just above the pub. If you take the path down to the left towards Godstow Lock, you can't miss the Godstow Abbey Ruins, a stunningly beautiful field of remains from an old Nunnery, walls and church intact. It is completely open, and you can go and look around, although it seems surreal when you find a cow standing in the middle of what was clearly the Abbey.

Working at The Trout was the most exciting albeit stressful nine months of my life. You'd have a tonne of fun, but the shifts were long and hard, either 10am-10pm or 12pm-whenever the last guests left with a 2- or 3-hour break in the middle. It wasn't long after I started when colleagues began saying things like, 'be careful of Rosie' or 'goodnight, Rosie', with completely straight faces, on their way upstairs to bed. Absolutely fascinated, I started asking about her and soon learned about Rosamund the Fair.

The legend has it that Rosamund the Fair (the King's mistress) was a young nun who lived in the Nunnery across the river Thames from The Trout. When the King would visit to have his shoes made, he would light a candle in the bedroom window facing the river to signal that it was safe for Rosie to come and pay him a secret visit.

Eventually the Queen found out about the King's escapades in Oxford, so she conjured a plan to catch Rosie in the act.

One cold evening, she visited Oxford herself and had her servants light a candle in the window. When Rosie later arrived, The Queen had her killed (possibly beheaded) and done away with in the river directly outside the building.

Rosie's ghost has lived in The Trout ever since.

Every person that has ever worked late at night or lived at The Trout recounts that when they first heard about Rosie, they thought it was just a funny story and a load of bollocks, frankly. However, their minds change very quickly given the right opportunity and time of day.

Rosie's modus operandi usually includes:
- Noises and echos
- Movement of objects
- Relighting fires or making fires more powerful
- Knocking
- Pushing objects off surfaces to make them fall
- Flicking glasses off shelves
- Cold spots in the 40s and 50s

95% of the interactions I've experienced with Rosie are between 2-4am, and more specifically, 3-3.30am. She is known to not like or be friendly towards men but oddly is happy to stop anything she's doing if you ask politely.

One of the managers I used to work with called Mia, was particularly friendly with Rosie and would always take the time to talk to her. If there were noises or objects moving around, Mia would say, 'I am starting to get a little scared now Rosie, if you could please stop that would make me a lot more comfortable', and everything would just … stop. We almost thought that Rosie enjoyed making Mia notice she was there - like a strange bond they had. One of her most regular games with Mia was to flash lights on and off vigorously.

My first personal experience was one evening after a very big business party that went until 2.30am in the 50s. This room is regularly used for parties because it is more private and doesn't disturb any other guests.

I had cleaned all the tables up and was setting the room up for the lunch service the next day. I had put all the cutlery neatly on the tables, a napkin, two forks and two knives at each place setting and went out to collect some freshly polished wine glasses from the bar. I was only out of the room long enough to load my fingers up with wine glass stems and when I returned, without a sound, all of the cutlery had been moved into neat little piles in the middle of each table. I froze completely, A shiver ran down my spine and I quickly yelled out, 'is anyone else back here?' with no response.

I ran outside to get a colleague who was working in the kitchen and asked him to stand with me a moment while I fixed and then finished the room.

The fireplace which had gone out around 45 minutes earlier had also started smoking again with a fresh ember.

My second and most haunting experience happened again around 3am after a big party in the 50s had gone home. My colleague Ash and I were the only staff left downstairs at the time. We were laughing whilst closing down the bar and cleaning the coffee machine as this party had gone particularly hard on espresso martinis. Suddenly we heard a soft screeching coming from down by the entryway to the 40s. We both looked up to see what was going on and heard the noise again, it sounded this time like a screeching dragging noise. Our faces dropped and right in front of our eyes, not fifteen metres away, a bar stool was dragging itself across the stone floor for about 1/2 a metre.

We didn't scream, but we both took a big step back and said, 'we are really scared Rosie, could you please stop?' and it did. Eyes affixed to the stool, Ash grabbed her mobile phone from her pocket and called up to the manager in the office to come down and be with us - we were terrified!

Other regular memories of mine include hearing whispers in the back rooms, walking up to side tables in the back rooms and watching things fall off before I got there, feeling a sense of severe unease when alone and pre-emptively taking a partner with me to reset rooms late at night. I got used to all of these things and started to embrace the encounters towards the end of my stay.

On one of my days off, Jonno (a colleague) was working a busy day at the bar when the majority of our guests were taking in the sunshine on the terrace. We didn't have any tables seated in the 40s or 50s this day but a young boy (about 12 years old) came up to the bar and asked Jonno who the lady in fancy dress was? Perplexed, Jonno replied that we don't have any fancy dress parties in today, thinking that it was a bit of a strange question and the boy replied, 'well she's standing up on the wall off the floor in the end room down there'. Upon further questioning she was described to have long dark hair, almost black, and was wearing a long white dress, 'like a nightgown'. Creepy!

Another manager, Andy, had many experiences of feeling shivers down his spine, described as something walking down his back, seeing things move and hearing voices late at night. In fact, the managers at The Trout are generally the best people to ask for their experiences because they are actively working the latest shifts to close the pub and set the alarms.

I went back to the UK to visit in July/August 2022 and was desperately sad to hear that since the renovations of The Trout over the COVID lockdowns, Rosie's activities have dramatically subsided or even ceased. I sincerely hope this is not the case and she is just taking a short holiday. Everyone I spoke with though had their own recounts of personal experiences with her.

The Trout is a fabulous place to enjoy some food/drink, soak in some history or do some casual celebrity spotting. But make sure to say, 'hi' to Rosie if you're ever lucky enough to visit."[44]

Heather's account provides us with a treasure trove of paranormal occurrences, in what must surely be one of the most haunted pubs in England, but I would personally be hesitant to "say hi to Rosie" if there's any truth to the legendary demise of a local game keeper, George Reid...

The story goes that sometime in the 1950s, George Reid returned home one evening and told his wife he had encountered a woman in a white robe. He said he stepped aside to let her pass, yet she seemed to glide by without any visible movement. He was certain it had been the ghost of Fair Rosamond. The very next day, Reid was found dead—face down in a puddle no more than two inches deep—on the exact same spot where the apparition had appeared.

Dead but Awake

15.
BLACK JACK'S HOLE

If you walk away from the ruins of Godstow and follow the riverbank across Port Meadow toward the city of Oxford, a short two-minute stroll will bring you to Godstow Lock—distinguished as the highest hydraulic-operated pound lock on the River Thames. The lock has been in operation since the 1790s. However, in 1787—before its final location was determined—there was considerable debate among the commissioners about whether to build the pound lock at an alternative site on the meadow, roughly one kilometre closer to the city. This area, known as Black Jack's Hole, may have been dismissed not just for practical reasons, but perhaps also due to superstition. Black Jack's Hole has long been associated with suicides, fatal accidents, ghostly sightings, and even tales of goblins.

It took some time to pinpoint the exact location of Black Jack's Hole, as it doesn't appear on any maps published after the 19th century. I had to consult crudely drawn Victorian-era maps and compare them with modern cartography and satellite imagery. I also enlisted the help of a few friends who live on canal boats to make local enquiries along the waterways.

I was mightily pleased when I finally managed to locate it. As it turns out, Black Jack's Hole lies along a stretch of the meadow I've walked across many times. Once a willowy island, it is now seamlessly embedded into meadow. Though this tranquil spot doesn't visibly stand out from the rest of Port Meadow, it is a place steeped in folklore.

Intrigued by the strange tales surrounding this otherwise unremarkable patch of land, I decided to delve into its past. My investigation began with a search of burial inquest records from the nearby St Sepulchre's churchyard. There, I uncovered two particularly intriguing deaths linked to Black Jack's Hole, both dating back to the mid-to-late 1800s...

The first report states the following.

"1863 - 1886 Edward Shonberg, Undergraduate at Exeter College who died in a boating accident at Black Jack's Hole on the Thames near Godstow"

On 18 February 1886, Edward Shonberg, an undergraduate at Exeter college, and another student, Mr Glover, dressed in their finest boating costumes and rowed along the Thames. Unfortunately, as they approached Black Jack's Hole, their vessel capsized, despite the efforts of other boaters, Edward could not be saved, Glover almost drowned himself, this was perhaps the least mysterious drowning at Black Jack's Hole as Shonberg and Glover were inexperienced boaters and neither could swim, which prompts the question, what on earth were they thinking? [45]

The second burial inquest record from St. Sepulchre's Cemetery, linked to Black Jack's Hole, reads as follows...

"1874- 1890 Reginald Arthur Clayton Hyslop

The fifteen-year-old son of a fraudulent Clergymen, who drowned in Black Jack's Hole on the Thames near Godstow when caught in weed whilst swimming."

I found it rather amusing that the fraudulent past of poor Reginald's clergyman father was mentioned in the official burial inquest, strange times, indeed.

Reginald, an attendant at the Bodleian library,

had taken a punt with three friends to their favourite swimming spot, which unfortunately happened to be Black Jack's Hole, poor Reginald apparently cried for help before vanishing under the water, his body was recovered an hour later, tangled up in weeds, people at the time were perplexed as to how a healthy young and strong swimmer would suddenly drown the way he did.[46]

After searching the archives of St Sepulchre's Cemetery, I turned to the British Newspaper Archives and discovered accounts of more mysterious deaths at Black Jack's Hole.

On 23 December 1908, newspapers reported that on the previous day, the body of twenty one year old Alice Titchener had been recovered from Black Jack's Hole, Titchener a servant at 74 Banbury road, had been missing from her work, strangely, she was found fully clothed and her hat, cloak and a purse containing some money were discovered on the bank.[47]

Despite being a known to friends and family as a person of a cheerful nature the jury returned a verdict of "suicide whilst of unsound mind'.

Almost exactly eleven years later, another twenty-one-year-old house servant drowned in Black Jack's Hole.

It was mid-December 1919 when Nellie Hubbocks and her sister Emma went for a Sunday evening stroll with two male acquaintances along the tow path of the river, Nellie had been on the arm of her soldier boyfriend when she slipped into the river, the party ran to the loch keeper who searched in vain for Nellie from a punt, her body wasn't recovered until the following day.[48]

And as recent as 21 June 2024, A group of Oxford university students celebrated their end of year exams by jumping into the water at Port Meadow from the Thames Path footbridge by Fiddler's Island, ominously very close to Black Jack's Hole.

Tragically a 19-year-old Brasenose student wearing full

academic dress jumped in and drowned before he could make it back to the bank.

At the time a spokesman for Thames Valley Police initially described the death as 'sudden' and 'unexplained'.[49]

But these are just a few among the many mysterious deaths that have taken place at Black Jack's Hole.

Just across the river, a few minutes' walk from Black Jack's Hole, stands a charming thatched tavern called The Perch, with a history dating back to the 12th century. This historic public house has witnessed its fair share of drama over the centuries, having survived two major fires—the most recent, in 2007, caused significant damage. Tradition has it that the pub is haunted by a sailor who lived in the parish of Binsey, who is believed to have drowned his sorrows before drowning himself in Black Jack's Hole.

Back in the 1970s, ghost story collector John Richardson documented a manifestation of the phantom sailor that was witnessed by several people. "One evening when the Inn was full of customers a figure dressed in old style naval uniform had approached the bar and ordered a drink. While the Landlord was in the process of pouring a pint the figure just disappeared from view. Other customers standing nearby were able to confirm the spectres disappearance.

It was only sometime later that the Landlord discovered that a petty officer had once lived in the neighbourhood and had frequented the Perch. This man had apparently got river himself into serious debt and had drowned in the river near by"[50]

Another variation of the legend is that the sailor was heartbroken over a failed relationship before plunging into the river.

I recently came across a fascinating book from 1909 that explores the history of the River Thames, *The Stripling Thames: a Book of The River Above Oxford*, the author, Fred

Thacker, had this to say of Black Jack's Hole.

> "Black jacks was once a willowy island, is now part of the meadow, the river is still very deep at black jacks ("Black Johns Pitt "in Wood) Though once much deeper, to scare youngsters from bathing there, a bogey tale was told them of an evil goblin who would leap upon them and keep them underwater in his cave."[51]

The burial inquests, along with the Victorian bogey tales, make it quite clear that Black Jack's Hole was long regarded as a hazardous place for any kind of river activity.

I recently read Marilyn Yurdan's excellent book; *Unexplained Oxford and Oxfordshire*, and came across an account that I found particularly compelling.

On 23 June 1971, a group of around twenty students from the College of Further Education (now Oxford and Cherwell College) gathered to celebrate the completion of their A-levels. They spent the evening drinking beer and cooking food over a bonfire on a scenic stretch of riverbank in Port Meadow. The spot they had chosen was directly across the river from The Perch Inn. It was such a clear night that they could see the pub in the distance, roughly 200 metres from where they were gathered.

A few hours into the celebrations, the group were joined by two guitar wielding students who had stopped in Oxford en route to interviews at the Royal College of Music in London. Their arrival sparked a lively singalong, and the merriment continued late into the night, well after The Perch Inn had closed. In fact, the party watched as the last of the pub's patrons sauntered out of the establishment. After a while, the party, in pockets of two and threes, slowly became aware of a solitary figure which had seemingly appeared out of no-where, a field away from where they sat, initially no one said a word as they watched the figure which moved oddly. Its motions were strangely smooth—gliding forward with no natural rise or fall as it travelled through the fields.

The party were astonished by the height of this figure, which towered well above the cows, it must have been around eight feet tall, it was uniformly grey with seemingly no facial features or limbs, only the head and shoulders could be defined.

The watching crowd rose from their feet in anticipation, breaking their silence as they acknowledged the presence of this strange figure to one another, then, for around two minutes, the crowd stood in curious silence, not so much scared, more fascinated, one member of the party with his arms in the shape of a cross, shouted at the entity "I'll cross it through it, blast me!", the boy's shouting seemed to grab the attention of the figure who turned to face the group before it slowly vanished, the members of the party stared in utter disbelief, one person made a note of the time, it was 12.05am.

A couple of strangers had joined the group a few minutes earlier, though the party were so caught up in the affair, no one had noticed them.

"So, you've seen it too then? ", asked the young man, the group, feigning ignorance, pressed the boy who eventually informed the group that his brother had witnessed the same entity a few days earlier.

A few evenings later, a few members of the party reunited and discussed the weird event, "I wonder what the date was the night we had the barbecue, and if there's any connection with what we saw?" asked one of the men, it transpired that the incident had taken place on 23 June, Midsummer's eve, a date of great spiritual relevance to many folks, a time when the pagans would traditionally light bonfires to scare away evil spirits and off course, this party had lit a bonfire.[52]

After studying the embankments proximity to the Perch Inn, I concluded that the party must have been gathered less than a five-minute walk from Black Jack's Hole and that the strange spectre must have headed from that obscure pretty field which harbours such a macabre past. Port Meadow is undeniably a sprawling paradise in Oxford but beware should you ever find yourself wandering through the tranquil fishing spot of Black Jack's Hole, a mysterious place associated with drownings, suicides, ghosts and goblins.

Dead but Awake

16.
THE GHOSTS OF LINCOLN COLLEGE

Founded in 1427, Lincoln College is reputed to be one of the most haunted colleges in Oxford. I've divided this chapter into three sections, each focusing on a different area of the college. The first two accounts come from old notes on Oxford ghosts, originally collected in the early 1990s by Oxford Guild of Tour Guides members Nuala Young and Eva Wagner, recently edited by Magnus Macfarlane, a gifted teller of ghost stories, The final account was given to me firsthand by Lincoln College's night porter in 2024.

THE ORGAN SCHOLAR

Every college has its own organ scholar and in the 1913, the scholar was a very popular individual and regarded as a wonderful organist. Everybody loved him, but he was called up to war and another young man had to take his place. The new organist was very nervous, He thought he was never going to match up to the previous one. He would like to go to the chapel at night to play the organ when nobody was listening. He really felt he was going to improve. One night though when he came to play, he was walking up to the chapel when he heard the organ playing already. He thought this was very strange - maybe the previous organist had come back on leave or something?

He went on to the door of the chapel, but the doors were locked, which was odd as he had just got the keys from the porter. He unlocked the door while the organ was still playing but it stopped as he opened it. He went into the chapel. There was no one to be seen at the organ, he looked around behind the tombs of the founders and other places to see if anyone was hiding, but nobody was there. He also felt that there was a notable chill in the air in the chapel. At that point he decided he would not practice that night and came out locking the doors behind him. As he walked away from the chapel, suddenly in the background, he heard the music start up again. He was spooked and wasn't going back in to check again. The next morning, when he gave the key back to the porter, he decided to mention his experience. The porter said that it might have been the previous organ scholar, having returned as he saw him the previous day, walking through the porter's lodge.

The very next day the college received a telegram which informed them that the previous organist had been killed in battle, on the very same day that he was seen by the porter and heard in the chapel![53]

LINCOLN'S CELLAR

It's common for young people, around the age of 16 or 17, to get a part time job for a bit of extra income, when I was fifteen, I made some money deflating bouncy castles in Liverpool, but that's a story for another book. In Oxford, however, many teenagers find more conventional jobs, often working in the University's bars. One such account tells of a girl who was eager to start earning her own money and was delighted when a friend mentioned she was leaving her job at the Lincoln College bar. Excited by the opportunity, she went for the interview and was thrilled to be offered the position. However, once she began working there, the reason behind the vacancy quickly became all too clear.

On the first night, everything seemed to go wrong, wine glasses would inexplicably topple over and shatter into pieces.

She was asked to go down to the cellar to fetch more

supplies. But as soon as she reached the bottom, she was suddenly overwhelmed—unable to breathe or move. Panic set in, and it was only after a tremendous struggle that she managed to get herself back upstairs. Later, shaken, she confronted her friend and asked, 'Why did you let me take your job?' Her friend quietly admitted that she, too, had experienced the same terrifying sensations whenever she went down into the cellar.

The two girls decided to investigate the history of the bar, they came across an account of a grisly event which had taken place during the English Civil war, on this occasion, the Royalists had captured around thirty parliamentarian officers and held them in the cellar. Unfortunately, they were so tightly packed in, that they were asphyxiated and died. The girls concluded that this was probably why they were having these horrendous experiences in the cellar.[54]

THE SHAKING TABLE

The Wesley Room at Lincoln College serves as a memorial to John Wesley, the founder of Methodism, it is a preserved space that honours his time there and in particular the meetings of the so called Holy Club, a group of young students who supported each other in their religious practices and in their studies.

It is interesting to note that the term "Methodist' was initially bestowed upon the group as a derisory nickname by students who mocked how seriously Wesley and the Holy Club took their faith, regardless of the insult behind the nickname, the term Methodist evidently struck a chord with Wesley, he clearly favoured being called a Methodist above the other name given to the group, "The Bible Moths".[55]

The Wesley Room, which is on the first floor, is said by one of the college porters to be the site of many strange occurrences, students have reported that a study table in the Wesley room has a tendency to suddenly shake violently.[56]

Is this the ghost of John Wesley, thumping his fists on the table whilst pontificating about the morally lax university? Is he still angry that he was forced to relinquish his fellowship at Lincoln when he married Molly Vazeille in 1751 (up until 1868, college fellows were not allowed to marry)? Although Wesley had a habit of leaving institutions under a cloud, he was banned from preaching in many churches throughout England due to his controversial views on what he called "Dead religion".

Curiously, John Wesley himself claimed that the old rectory in Epworth, Lincolnshire, where he grew up, was haunted by a poltergeist, between December 1716 and January 1717 most of the Wesley family had reported encounters with this mischievous spirit, their accounts included phantasmal knockings, rattling chains, disembodied groans and violent door slamming.

The Wesley family even resorted to buying a fierce dog, a mastiff, in the hope it might scare away the ghost, unfortunately it would transpire that the dog was terrified of the ghost and hid under a table whenever things went bump in the night.

The Wesley family nicknamed the ghost "Old Jeffrey." Interestingly, it was also referred to as "The Wesley Poltergeist". Could it be, then, that John Wesley himself is the new Wesley Poltergeist?[57]

17.
THE SAXON TOWER AND THE SCARED MEDIUM

St Michael at the Northgate, located on Oxford's Cornmarket Street, is a beautiful church steeped in history. Its ancient Saxon tower stands tall and dignified, heroically holding its ground amid a sea of tacky Harry Potter shops and fast-food outlets. The church has welcomed figures such as John Wesley, who preached there, and textile designer William Morris, who married Jane Burden within its walls. In more recent years, it has also played host to performances by the renowned jazz guitarist Lulo Reinhardt.

The Saxon Tower, Oxfords oldest building.
{Photograph} Tom McDonnell

Every day, a steady stream of sightseers climb the tower for a bird's-eye view from the top, but a few years ago, within a very short span of time, three different people claimed to have felt an invisible but oppressive force pushing up against them as they made their way up the stairs, one woman even ran back down in a panic and told the tower keeper, 'I'm a medium—and there's definitely a spirit on those stairs. I'm not going back up there again!'

One of the tower keepers, Simon Ballard, whose colleague was alerted about the ghost by the medium, wryly pointed out that this was basically the equivalent of a firefighter refusing to do his job… because there was a fire![58]

It is difficult to pinpoint the source of the sinister force that frightened even a medium. While many prisoners met horrific ends in the long-gone Bocardo Prison, which once stood nearby, the Saxon tower itself was never part of the prison. But the tower will soon be a thousand years old, it is Oxford's oldest building—a silent witness to countless hidden stories and secrets that may never come to light.

18.
A PERMANENT RESIDENT AT THE EASTGATE HOTEL

The Eastgate Hotel on Merton Lane is a converted 17th-century coaching inn. In Saxon times, Oxford's boundaries were marked by a protective wall, and the hotel now stands where the east gate of that wall once existed.

In the summer of 2024, I spoke with Sahana, a woman who had worked at the Eastgate Hotel between April and December 2022. During her time there, she stayed in a room on the first floor—or at least tried to sleep there. She described frequently hearing strange noises outside her room: creaking floorboards, and more disturbingly, unsettling groaning sounds that had no clear source (it definitely wasn't a couple on honeymoon if that's what you're thinking).

Sahana told me that hotel guests often reported finding a towel mysteriously left outside their room, this seemingly random placement was believed to mark the room for a visit from the resident ghost.

According to Sahana, "Unless it was clearly someone from housekeeping, the best advice was not to open the door. If you hear a noise outside and choose to open it, you're essentially inviting the ghost into your room. The sounds outside the room varied—it could be a faint scratch at the door, a soft knock, or, on rare occasions, the ringing of a bell."

Sahana continued, "If the ghost did manage to enter the room, something would inevitably go wrong—a kettle would suddenly stop working, or the plumbing would mysteriously fail."

The ghost was said to be a friendly spirit, although one evening a chap called Placido, a manager at the hotel, went into the basement to change the beer barrels and claimed that an invisible force had pushed him down the stairs.

According to Bradley, a long-term employee, the ghost is believed to be that of an elderly woman who lived at the hotel many years ago—and it seems she has no intention of checking out any time soon.[59]

19.
PARANORMAL ACTIVITY AT THE SHELDONIAN

In September 1666, the Great Fire of London brought unimaginable destruction to the capital. Once the smoke had cleared, the city faced the daunting task of rebuilding. The astronomer and architect Sir Christopher Wren was chosen to lead this effort. His vision transformed London. The city was moulded into a style in line with the great European cities of the time, cities such as Rome and Paris, places that Wren had studied in exhaustive detail, however, in 1664, two years before Wren began reshaping London, construction was already underway in Oxford on what would become his second masterpiece: the Sheldonian Theatre. Serving as the university's graduation hall, the building wouldn't look out of place in the heart of Rome. In fact, having visited the Theatre of Marcellus in Rome, it is clear that it served as a strong source of inspiration for Wren.

The primary financial backer of the Sheldonian Theatre wasn't the university itself, but its chancellor, Gilbert Sheldon, the eponymous patron of the graduation hall.

Before the Sheldonian was built, graduation ceremonies, perhaps surprisingly, were held at the University Church of St Mary's. Gilbert Sheldon believed it was inappropriate to host such lively, often boisterous events in a sacred place of worship.

Within five years, Wren's iconic domed building was completed. Although not a theatre in the traditional sense, the Sheldonian serves as the venue for all major public ceremonies of the University. It regularly hosts concerts, musicals, and lectures by high-profile authors and politicians. I remember walking past the building on 27

August 2019, and being startled to see snipers positioned on nearby rooftops. My surprise made much more sense when I later learned that the speaker that day was Salman Rushdie.

The Sheldonian Theatre is also believed to be haunted. Over the years, an unusually high number of witnesses have reported a wide range of strange and unexplained occurrences within its walls.

In Marilyn Yurdan's *Unexplained Oxford and Oxfordshire*, several such reports are documented. However, since its publication in 1984, Marilyn has uncovered additional accounts of phantasmal activity at the theatre. I'm very grateful to her for generously sharing these later discoveries with me.

Before I delve into the incidents that occurred after 1984, I'll briefly touch on the sightings documented in Marilyn's book. Since these events are already thoroughly covered in *Unexplained Oxford and Oxfordshire*, what follows is simply a brief overview.

Pre-1985 Sightings

On one occasion, the assistant custodian claimed to have witnessed heavy prints vanish only to see them reappear moments later, another incident involved an electrician who had been hired to rewire the building, whilst performing his tasks. he sheepishly complained that he felt as though someone was continuously watching him at work.

Brian, the chief custodian at the time, reported a number of strange events, on one occasion he heard a phantom voice calling his name on the staircase, a voice which he claimed was distinctively female, a week or so later, alone in the theatre, Brian caught a glimpse of something dashing around the door, it seemed to be the frilly hem of a dress, on two other occasions he saw blue flashes which emanated from the locked upper gallery.[60]

Paranormal Reports From 1985 Onwards

Over the years, various members of staff have reported hearing mysterious footsteps, which sound as though someone is running, the footsteps are heard not only along the corridors but also on the staircases, they are usually heard late at night whilst the custodians are closing the building after a concert.

In her own words, this is a report from Marilyn in her capacity as Assistant Custodian of the Sheldonian.

> "During degree ceremonies and concerts, we used to have all the gallery doors open of course but always locked the one leading to the attic floor and then to the cupola. One afternoon the public had left, and we'd locked all the outer doors, so I went up to lock the gallery doors and unlock the cupola. As I started to go up, I could hear light footsteps going on ahead of me. I thought, well you're out of luck as you can't get much further. I kept going and so did they and all the time I was expecting them to turn round and that I'd meet whoever it was on their way down again. However, when I got to the top, the barrier was still across and the door securely locked. This made me laugh, and I called out, 'Okay, you win!' I checked out both the galleries on the way down but of course they were empty and locked."

Marilyn was later told the following account by the cleaner.

> "One morning the cleaner told me that when

he'd unlocked and gone into the auditorium, he'd caught sight of a young girl sitting in the Ladies' Gallery, just to the left of the doorway where the picture disappeared, and Brian heard his name called. From his description it sounded as if the young girl was wearing early-19th-century clothes, with a small hat, but as he looked at her, she rapidly disintegrated."[61]

Those who claim to have encountered her agree on one thing: the Sheldonian Theatre is definitely haunted by the spirit of a young girl; interestingly, witnesses have never felt threatened by the spectral girls presence, however, I am afraid that her identity may always be a mystery, neither myself nor Marilyn could dig up anything which lends the slightest clue to her identity. The thought did cross my mind that a séance might offer some answers but perhaps it's best to leave her in peace, free to skip quietly through the corridors and play her games of hide and seek with the theatre's custodians.

20.
LOCKED OUT OF MY HOUSE

On 20 January 2023, I interviewed a man from Folkestone named P Heaney as part of a project exploring his cousin's connections to the world of show business. During our conversation, I happened to mention *Dead but Awake*, and Paul responded by sharing a series of strange incidents that had occurred in a house he once lived in on Oatlands Road, near Oxford Train Station.

At the time, Heaney was living in the house with his elderly mother. On one night, he got up to fetch a glass of water. As he reached out to open the living room door, it was suddenly yanked away from him with surprising force. Startled, he instinctively assumed it was his mother—until he realised there was no one else there.

After Heaney's' mother passed away, the strange occurrences continued. The front door of the house was secured with a bolt on the inside, yet on two separate occasions, Heaney returned home to find himself locked out. The bolt had somehow slid into place, despite no one else being in the house. Each time, he had no choice but to kick the door in to regain entry.

A friend offered a rational explanation, suggesting that vibrations from passing lorries might have shifted the bolt. But Heaney quickly dismissed the theory: the house stood on a no-through road, and even if it hadn't, it was highly unlikely that heavy goods vehicles would be rumbling through a quiet residential street, especially in the evening. Something else, he felt certain, was responsible.

To this day, Heaney has no idea who—or what—the presence might have been, but he finished our conversation by telling me...

"I never believed in ghosts before then, I do now".[62]

Dead but Awake

21.
A DRAMA AT THE PLAYHOUSE

On November 14, 2023, I attended a fantastic event at the Oxford Playhouse Theatre: *Uncanny – I Know What I Saw*, hosted by the BBC's resident ghost expert, Danny Robins. The show explored recent claims of ghost sightings, with a panel of both sceptics and believers offering their perspectives. As I sat in the theatre, watching the dramatic reenactments—complete with eerie sound effects and atmospheric lighting—I couldn't help but think they had chosen the perfect venue, given the Playhouse's own reputation for being haunted.

Located on Oxford's Beaumont Street, just a short walk from the city centre, the theatre is a 663-seat, independently owned auditorium. Rumours suggest it may harbour a resident ghost, with several unexplained occurrences reported over the years.

Traces of the original Playhouse Theatre can still be found just a five-minute walk from its current location, at 12 Woodstock Road. Originally known as the Red Barn when it opened in 1923, the theatre later moved to its present site. The current Playhouse Theatre was officially opened in the 1930s by Irish actor and theatre manager J.B. Fagan, following the completion of its construction.

During the 1970s, numerous sightings were reported of an apparition drifting through the theatre. Witnesses described the ghost as a figure clad in white, her face obscured by a thin veil. She would come to be known as the White Nun.

In April 1978, the now-defunct newspaper, *The Oxford Journal* reported a sighting made by Miss F.D, a cleaning lady at the Playhouse.

According to the report, Miss F.D. was collecting her

equipment from the theatre's basement one morning when she was startled by a white spectre, its face concealed by a veil. She claimed the ghost floated through one of the cellar walls, drifted silently past her, and vanished through the opposite wall, as this was far from being the first sighting of the white lady, intrigued members of staff decided to investigate.

The staff would have been aware that the basement pre-dated the construction of the Playhouse in the 1930s, they were keen to discover what occupied the space before the theatre was built…[63]

After conducting my own research, I arrived at the same conclusion as the Playhouse staff did back in the 1970s—what unfolds is a story of kings, wars, and holy men.

Around 1130, King Henry I ordered the construction of Beaumont Palace—an enormous residence that would have stretched the entire length of what is now Beaumont Street. Situated just seven miles from the royal hunting grounds at Woodstock, the palace offered a convenient place for the king to rest.

Between 1133 and 1167, Beaumont Palace was the birthplace of three notable English monarchs—Henry II, Richard I, and King John—making it a site of great historical importance to the Crown. During the Battle of Bannockburn in 1314, a desperate Edward II prayed to the Virgin Mary, vowing that if he survived, he would found a monastery for the Carmelite order. True to his word, he fulfilled this promise in 1318 by granting Beaumont Palace to the Carmelite friars. However, the monastery was permanently closed during the dissolution of the monasteries in the 1530s. Could it be, then, that the pale spectre said to haunt the nearby Playhouse is not a white lady as commonly believed, but the ghost of a Carmelite friar? The Carmelites traditionally wore white robes and were often referred to as the White Friars. [64]

As Eva Wagner once told me, "It can be difficult to identify the gender and type of ghosts in Oxford, given that the flowing gowns worn by students often resemble the robes of monks and priests. Most of Oxford's ghosts seem to be dressed in cloaks and long, billowing garments."[65]

We may never know for certain whether the ghost of the 'White Nun' is, in fact, the spirit of a Carmelite friar- but there is undeniably a female presence said to haunt the theatre. Over the past few decades, Playhouse staff, including my friend Paul, who once worked there as a barman, have occasionally reported the sudden appearance of a mysterious fragrance, a sweet, rose-scented perfume that drifts through the air. Eerily, the scent is never accompanied by any visible presence.[66]

Dead but Awake

22.
THE POLTERGEIST OF ST EDMUND HALL

St Edmund Hall is a beautiful college with its first recorded mention dating back to 1317, though it likely existed even earlier. Medieval halls like St Edmund were established in Oxford to house and educate undergraduates. As the last surviving medieval hall, St Edmund Hall can claim to be "the oldest continuously operating academic society dedicated to housing and educating undergraduates at any university."

The Crypt, believed to date from the 1130s, was likely once a reliquary, though some speculate it may have served as a charnel house.

Many comedians such as Terry Jones, Stuart Lee and Al Murray the pub landlord, have studied at St Edmunds, but it's no laughing matter when it comes the college poltergeist.

There is a legend that in the 1960s, a dining hatch dramatically flew open, and a collection of glasses spectacularly imploded,[67] this was said to be the work of a malignant ghost, the identity of which seems to be a mystery, but it could possibly be linked to the ghost of a hanging boy which tradition has it, appears on a staircase, and is believed to be the ghost of a student who committed suicide, I have heard the legend of the hanging boy many times, it is also listed in the Paranormal Database, where anyone can submit their sightings, I haven't found any reports of a suicide at the college, although the university has always been extremely discreet about such matters. Personally, I know of a few suicides at Oxford that never made it into the newspapers.[68]

Interestingly, over the years, many St Edmund Hall

alumni have shown a fascination with the paranormal. For example, the St Edmund Hall Magazine from 1951-1952 reports that at the 501st meeting of the student society during Michaelmas term, E.J. Morgan opened the session with his essay *Brainwaves*, which examined paranormal phenomena like telepathy and clairvoyance from "a serious and intellectual standpoint," highlighting scientific experiments in the field. Later that term, E.L. Cunnel presented his essay *Things That Go Bump in the Night*, approaching the topic from "a low brow and sensational aspect and analysing our favourite ghosts and poltergeists". During the discussion that followed, members had the chance to share and debate their own "funny peculiar stories."[69]

One peculiar story, or legend to be concise, centres on an exorcism rumoured to have taken place at St Edmund Hall in the 1960's, a time frame which ties in with the imploding glasses and swinging hatch doors. Like suicides, exorcisms in Oxford colleges would almost certainly have been kept under wraps. There may well be some truth to this story, especially considering that Father Jeremy Davies, the chief exorcist for the Catholic Church in England and Wales, studied at St Edmund's.

Davies initially studied English at Oxford before switching to medicine, a path he eventually abandoned when he felt that he was "being called by God", he served as an assistant priest in London, until the cardinal appointed him as an exorcist, he would spend the rest of his career ritualistically expelling demons and the devil from people and buildings. [70]

In 2008, the Catholic Truth Society published Davies's paper *Exorcism: Understanding Exorcism in Scripture and Practice.* His views were notably uncompromising. He went so far as to link promiscuity to a rise in demonic possession, and he viewed practices such as alternative medicine and reading horoscopes as potentially dangerous gateways for demonic influence. According to Davies...

"The thin end of the wedge (soft drugs, yoga for relaxation, horoscopes just for fun and so on) is more dangerous than the thick end because it is more deceptive – an evil spirit tries to make his entry as unobtrusively as possible."

Davies added .."Beware of any claim to mediate beneficial energies (e.g. reiki), any courses that promise the peace that Christ promises (e.g. enneagrams), any alternative therapy with its roots in eastern religion (e.g. acupuncture)."[71]

In a funny twist of fate, when Father Davies died in December 2022, his obituary was penned by his nephew, Nick Davies, a self-described "atheist, yoga-loving former Guardian reporter".[72]

With such an uncompromising and hardline worldview, it's little wonder the Church entrusted Father Jeremy Davies with the task of confronting demons. Frankly, he scares the hell out of me—pun very much intended.

Dead but Awake

23.
THE PHANTOMS OF TRINITY COLLEGE

Trinity College is truly iconic. Its alumni include three prime ministers—Frederick North, William Pitt, and Spencer Compton—as well as playwright Terence Rattigan and theologian John Henry Newman. It also holds a place in fiction, being the college, the enigmatic Jay Gatsby claimed to have attended in F. Scott Fitzgerald's masterpiece, *The Great Gatsby*. Film and television enthusiasts may also recognise Trinity as a key location in the acclaimed 1980s adaptation of *Brideshead Revisited*.

Trinity was founded in 1555 by Sir Thomas Pope, a catholic lawyer who had amassed great wealth in his role as Treasurer of the Court of Augmentations, the court's function was to establish better control over land and capital which up until the Dissolution of the Monasteries had belonged to the Roman Catholic church, Pope achieved great influence in his position as Treasurer.

Although he married three times, none of his unions produced children. With no sons or daughters to pray for his soul, he stipulated in the statutes of Trinity College that the students were to remember him in their prayers. While this might seem like an odd request today, it reflected the deeply religious—and turbulent—times in which he lived. Sir Thomas Pope, a devout Catholic, had served in government under Henry VIII. Yet Trinity College was founded during the reign of Mary I, whose chief priority was the restoration of the Catholic Church's dominance in England.

Trinity College was built on the site of a former Benedictine monastery, once home to monks from Durham. Remnants of the original monastery remain part of the college to this day—including the old library beside the chapel. And as for the chapel itself, many believe it to be haunted.

The chapel at Trinity is one of the smallest in Oxford, yet undeniably one of the most beautiful. Built in 1696 by Dean Henry Aldrich, with guidance from none other than Christopher Wren, its interior is adorned with spectacular woodcarvings by the Dutch master Grinling Gibbons—arguably the greatest wood craftsman who ever lived. Wren himself was said to be astonished by Gibbons' extraordinary talent. Look up, and you're rewarded with Pierre Berchet's *Christ in Glory*, a breathtaking 17th-century painting that celebrates the triumph of Christ after the resurrection. But according to legend, not all resurrections associated with this quaint chapel have been holy.

One morning in 1959, around 10 a.m., the verger—Mr. H—was carrying out his usual ritual of dusting the pews in the chapel when he was suddenly overcome by the unmistakable feeling that he was not alone. Trusting his instincts, he slowly turned… and there she was. A woman dressed in black stood before him, her expression serene, her smile warm and familiar. And then, as swiftly as she had appeared, she vanished—gone in the blink of an eye.

Perplexed and deeply moved, Mr. H couldn't shake the feeling that he knew the smiling apparition. Later that day, it came to him: it was his late mother. But she appeared much younger than he remembered her at the end of her life, … The verger's heart was warmed by this visitation.

Seven years later, in 1966, another strange event occurred at the chapel, sadly this event was of a tragic nature, the organ had recently been rebuilt thanks to the generosity of Sir Harry Brittain, and a special service was held to celebrate its restoration, All seemed well—until the conclusion of the first hymn. A sudden scream pierced the

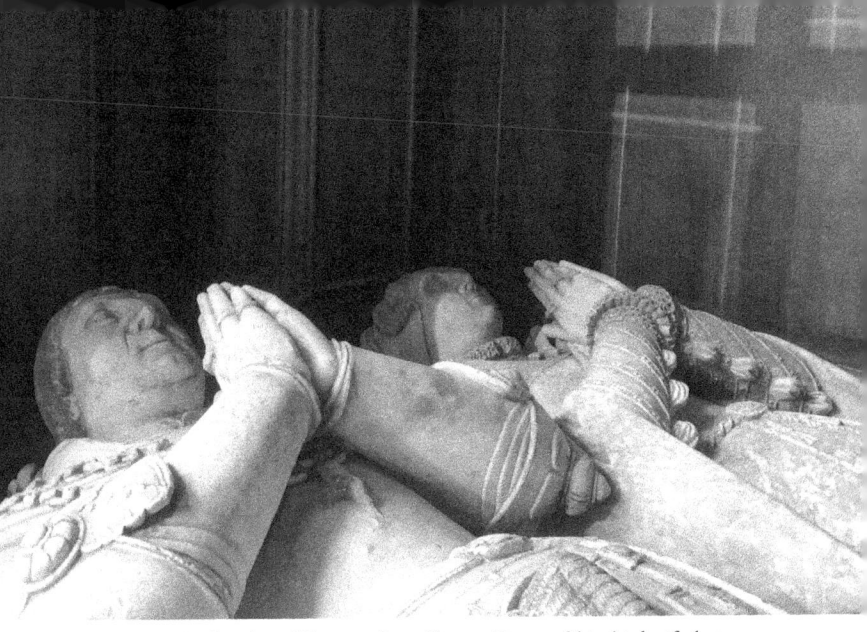

A memorial to the founder of Trinity college, Thomas Pope and his third wife, but are they really resting in peace?
{Photograph} Tom McDonnell

air, followed by the chilling sound of a single organ note, held far too long.

The verger rushed to investigate and was met with a harrowing sight: the young organist slumped over the keys, lifeless. He had suffered a massive heart attack, his face frozen in an expression of absolute terror. The unexpected death of an otherwise healthy young man once again reignited rumours of supernatural forces at work in the chapel.

But the chapel is not the only haunted building in Trinity, if one was to peer through the iron blue gates of Trinity, your eyes would automatically be drawn to The West tower which looms majestically on the far side of the front lawn, at the top of the tower stand four female statues which represent astronomy, geometry, music and medicine, it is without question an impressive edifice, however, some strange events have occurred inside the tower. In late October, 2020, I stood outside the iron gates of Trinity and conversed with a man called Russell, he was the assistant archivist of Trinity and former college carpenter, as it was close to Halloween our conversation turned to that of ghosts, Russell informed me that over the years various people had claimed to have heard unaccompanied footsteps throughout the building, [73]

There is a persistent rumour that the invisible footsteps belong to the ghost of Thomas Pope's third wife, Elizabeth Blount. According to tradition, when her apparition is seen, she appears without her legs, one explanation for this peculiar manifestation is architectural: the floor levels have been raised over the centuries, and Elizabeth is said to wander on the level of the original floor.

But who was Elizabeth Blount, and why would she haunt Trinity college?

Elizabeth was a lady from illustrious stock, a relative of Robert Dudley, the Earl of Leicester, According to one of her acquaintances, Sir Thomas Pope was moved to take her as his third wife largely because of her charitable nature and "other excellent qualities.", Elizabeth, for her part, was said to be impressed by Pope's honourable vision of founding a college. Ironically, their marriage was officiated by Archbishop Thomas Cranmer, the very same Protestant reformer who would later be burned at the stake on the orders of Queen Mary I, just across the road from the newly founded Trinity College.[74]

Sir Thomas Pope died in January 1559, and Elizabeth outlived him by thirty-four years. I found myself wondering what became of her after his death. As I delved deeper into her story, I was initially sceptical of the claim that she is the ghost said to haunt Trinity's West Tower, but the more I read, the less certain I became.

In December 1559, around ten months after Pope's death, Emily remarried. Her new husband, Sir Hugh Powlett, was a very different kettle of fish from Pope the political administrator. Sir Hugh was a powerful, swashbuckling soldier and courtier, a man whose numerous exploits could easily fill an entire book. A brief overview of his achievements reveals his deep favour with Henry VIII, who held him in such high regard that he was invited to attend the baptism of Prince Edward. Powlett was later knighted by the king for his gallant service against the French during the reign of Edward VI. He also served as Marshal of the army that crushed the rebels of Cornwall and Devonshire. Later; serving Queen Elizabeth, he successfully defended Newhaven from French attack.[75]

Emily's new life with Sir Hugh must have taken some adjustment. He had fought in so many battles that the possibility of being widowed a second time must surely have crossed her mind. Yet, as I discovered, Dame Elizabeth Powlett—as she came to be known, did not let the demands of her new life distract her from her responsibilities as the foundress of Trinity College. Her late husband had entrusted her with full authority over the nomination of scholars and the management of many financial aspects of the college.

It was highly unusual for a woman of her time to wield such influence in an Oxford institution, but Elizabeth exercised this power with confidence and determination until the end of her life. She even brought Sir Hugh on board, enlisting his support in safeguarding the interests of the college.

The scholars fortunate enough to be admitted to Trinity under Elizabeths direction were naturally grateful. One of them, Sir Edward Hoby, who would go on to become an important statesman, later described her as 'Praeno bilis heroina', …A very noble heroine[76]

A curious incident took place in 1560, Elizabeth arranged for a richly painted glass pane to be inserted in a window of a chancel in the church of Broadwell,

Oxfordshire, the glass depicted an image of the Holy Trinity with her and Thomas Pope kneeling in their heraldic coat of arms, a year later she arranged for the same window to be destroyed, being censured as superstitious, probably because she had recently married Sir Hugh. [77]

Elizabeth passed away in Hertfordshire on 27 October 1593. Five days later, her body arrived in Oxford and was laid in state at the University Church of St Mary. The following day, her remains were carried down the road to Trinity College, where she was interred in the chapel alongside Sir Thomas and his first previous spouse, Margaret.

The service was attended by scholars, fellows and the college president, all whom were clothed in mourning attire which had been paid for by Dame Elizabeth herself, also present were twenty-five of the poorest women who could be found in Oxford, these destitute women were ordered to attend the ceremony and were clothed in black habits. It was Elizabeth's wish that all of the attendants, regardless of rank, dined together at Trinity's Dining Hall, we can only imagine what the haughtier members of the college thought of this request, any remains from the sumptuous feast were given to the poor at the gates of Trinity.[78]

Dame Elizabeths devotion to the development and success of Trinity continued decades after Sir Thomas Popes death, after discovering her wish to be interred at the college, combined with her passion for the place, I have come to the conclusion that it would be quite fitting if she does haunt the college, eternally roaming the grounds of Trinity, which she clearly held great affection for.

But there may well be yet another ghost at Trinity. An old friend of mine, Jules, once told me about a strange incident that unsettled one of the college's waitresses back in 2016. Jules had heard the story from Omar, a man who worked at the college.

It happened in the Warden's Room, where a buzzer is used to call staff for food and drink service. One day, the buzzer went off unexpectedly. A newly employed waitress arrived with a tray, only to find the door locked—which was odd, since the door could only be locked from the outside. Concerned that someone might have been accidentally shut in, she called for the porters to unlock it.

But when they opened the door, the room was completely empty.

Everyone involved recalled how deeply the experience unsettled her. She had only just begun working at Trinity—and decided to leave soon after.[79]

Before we move on from Trinity, I must mention Artemis, the resident cat of Trinity college, he seems to have been around for years, he is a lovely black cat who enjoys gate crashing other colleges and on occasion likes to follow me around Oxford!

People of a superstitious predisposition have been known to be wary of black cats, I believe that it's always worth reminding these people of an observation made by that great philosopher of the last century, Groucho Marx

"If a black cat crosses your path… it signifies that the animal is going somewhere"

Dead but Awake

24.
AMY, THE WANDERING GHOST

In 1560, Queen Elizabeth I sat on the throne of England and was rumoured to be in love with a man known for his charm, intelligence, and, above all, ruthlessness, Robert Dudley, the Earl of Leicester. The so-called Virgin Queen was imprudent enough to give the impression that she wished to marry him. However, Dudley was already married to a woman of relatively high social standing: Amy Robsart.

Amy lived four miles west of Oxford city in a large house called Cumnor Hall, it is believed that she did not leave her house once during the entire summer of 1560, the reason behind this eremitic behaviour is unclear, some believe she was too depressed to leave the house, disconsolate over her husband's passion for the Queen, others speculate that she was too sick to leave her home, this view was corroborated by rumours at court which suggested she was suffering from "a malady in her breast".[80]

On 8 September, the day of the St Michaelmas fair, Amy ordered all of her staff to leave Cumnor Hall and attend the fair in the nearby market town of Abingdon, Amy refused to attend the fair herself, when the staff returned at night, they made a grim discovery, poor Amy lay lifeless at the bottom of a staircase, she had fallen a mere six steps, her neck had snapped like a twig, she was only twenty-eight years old.

Her death aroused suspicion, rumours circulated that Dudley may have had his wife killed so he could legitimately propose to the Queen.

There has been some speculation that Amy took her own life, but this is highly unlikely. In 16th-century England, suicide was considered a serious crime. Victims were denied a Christian funeral and, by law, were to be buried anonymously by the roadside. Their heirs would be stripped of their inheritance, which would instead go to the Crown. There was also the terrifying prospect of eternal damnation, as taking one's own life was deemed unforgivable by the Church. Amy, known to be deeply religious and a woman of frequent prayer, would have been acutely aware of these consequences.[81]

One might also argue that there are easier and more certain ways to take one's own life than by throwing oneself down a staircase.

The Queens advisers began to view Dudley with suspicion, Elizabeth was cautioned to keep a distance from Dudley, a man now regarded as potentially dangerous, possibly a wife killer, it is fair to assume that Elizabeth was well aware of how brutally cruel men could be to their wives, her father's actions would have served as a constant reminder.

Dudley's cause was not helped by his reputation for skulduggery, he was an ambitious master courtier with many foes, when he founded the Oxford University Press, it was developed under his guidance to churn out anti- Catholic propaganda, the consequence of this action naturally led to an increase of enemies, secretive enemies who worked tirelessly to sully his reputation.

Dudley also had Protestant enemies, in 1598, a decade after Amy's death, Privy council member Lord Burghley coughed and spluttered on his death bed, utterly convinced Dudley had poisoned him, moments before he succumbed, he apparently had this to say of Dudley, "Beware the Gypsy for he is too hard for you all, you know not the nature of the beast as well as I do".

There is some speculation that Elizabeth may have been complicit in Amy's downfall, the Spanish Ambassador openly spread gossip he'd heard at court, that the

Queen and Dudley "were thinking of destroying lord Robert's wife", he also claimed the Queen had told him discreetly that "Lady Roberts was dead- or nearly so", the Ambassador claimed he was told this information four days prior to Amy's demise.

Court rumours aside, Elizabeth did distance herself from Dudley for many years, a move which stifled his political ambitions, Dudley would never achieve his dream of marrying his Queen, besides, there was a rival for her love that he could not compete with, a rival the Queen often mentioned, in a phrase she often repeated, "I am already bound unto a husband… which is the Kingdom of England."

Amy Dudley was laid to rest on 22 September 1560, two weeks after her death, at the University Church of St Mary the Virgin. For the occasion, an intricately carved hearse had been set up inside the church to receive her coffin. The chief mourner was Lady Margery Norris, a close friend of the Queen. The funeral was a lavish spectacle, costing Robert Dudley over £2,000—equivalent to around £810,000 today, no expense was spared.[82]

Which makes it all the more surprising then, that with the passage of time, Amy's grave in the chancel of St Mary's Church gradually faded from memory. After a fire in 1946, excavations were carried out in the chancel, revealing that additional vaults had been constructed in the 18th and 19th centuries. The entire floor had been completely disturbed at some point after Amy's death and burial.[83]

Today, a small marble tile set into the chapel floor is all that remains to mark her resting place—but it is said that Amy's ghost serves as a more permanent reminder.

Various choirs perform concerts at St Marys including Christchurch and Magdalen college boys' school choirs, tradition has it, that occasionally, a choir boy will report a

Dead but Awake

The Memorial to Amy Robsart in the church she is said to wander.
{Photograph} Tom McDonnell

sighting of a woman drifting around, not just inside the church, but sometimes on the front lawn, she is said to be tall and elegant with a sad demeanour.

It seems that only children have seen her apparition on the grounds of the church, perhaps children have a higher sense of awareness for such things, an awareness unspoilt by the cynicism which naturally accompanies adulthood.[84]

Although the small memorial reminds us that Amy was laid to rest in the chapel, she may well be the most restless spirit in Oxford. There's a reason I titled this chapter The Wandering Ghost—she is said to have been seen in various parts of the county.

Sightings of Amy's ghost were even reported during Robert Dudley's lifetime, these reports strengthened the public's perception that Amy was murdered, it was claimed her ghost had been seen on the steps she had tumbled down in Cumnor Hall, her apparition continued to haunt the area long after the house had been torn down, in an attempt to give peace to her tormented soul, a curious exorcism was performed, one which required the efforts of no less than twelve clergymen, her spirit was somehow transferred into an old water feature at Cumnor place, known as "Lady Dudley's pond". According to legend, the pond hasn't frozen since.

Although it seems that Amy's restless spirit has resisted the efforts of those twelve men of God, there is another intriguing supernatural tale linking her to a pub in Cumnor called The Vine Inn. At one time, a portrait of Amy Robsart hung on the wall there.

During the war, a group of service personnel gathered at the pub, including a member of the Women's Auxiliary Air Force who, coincidentally, was also named Amy. She appeared in every group photograph taken—except in those where the portrait of Amy Robsart was also visible.

It seems however, that The Vine Inn is not the only Cumnor pub frequented by Amy, in August 2013, a Marion S, had this to say on trip advisor about his stay at The Bear and Ragged Staff.

"Late in the night, at about two o'clock, we woke startled because the tv sprang to life. I shut it off at the tv itself but again it started to blink. I pulled the plug to make an end to the spectacle. When I mentioned it to the proprietor, he humorously told me that it probably was the ghost of Amy Robsart (Robert Dudley's wife) who had died across the street".[85]

Amy is also rumoured to haunt Worcester College—known in the 16th century as Gloucester Hall—on Beaumont Street. The doors at either end of a great hall are said to open and close in sequence, just far enough apart for someone to pass through. That someone is believed to be Amy herself, whose body was once laid out in the hall before her burial at the University Church.

The idyllic setting of Wytham, around seven kilometres

Lady Dudley's Pond in Cumnor, said to never freeze, is rumoured to hold the spirit of Amy Robsart.
{Photograph} Tom McDonnell

from Oxford city centre, is also rumoured to be one of Amy's haunts.

As a child, my friend Adam spent a few months living in Wytham Abbey, the building consisted of modern flats connected by ancient stone corridors. Adam remembered it as a lovely place to live, though at times it could feel a little eerie — he would sometimes get the unsettling sensation that someone was walking just behind him. Later, a neighbour told him of a local rumour: that the bannisters in Wytham Abbey had been taken from Amy's House in Cumnor, Adam dismissed this as hearsay—at least until 9 August 2025, when I came across a print of an old picture from 1821. The image depicted... *Windows & doorway at Wytham Abbey, Berks removed from Cumnor Place, Oxon*

This discovery makes it seem highly likely that the bannisters at Wytham Abbey were also taken from Amy's house.[86]

There has also been speculation that Amy's vengeful spirit may have played a role in Robert Dudley's demise. In 1588—twenty-eight years after her death—Amy's ghost is said to have wandered thirteen miles from Cumnor to Cornbury Park.

At the time, Dudley was on the grounds of the vast estate, indulging in his favourite pastime: hunting in the Wychwood Forest. During the hunt, he was suddenly struck by a mysterious illness. The following day, as he lay on what would become his deathbed, he reportedly recalled seeing Amy approaching him in the forest, Dudley claimed that his dead wife uttered these ominous words, "In ten days thou will be with me".[87]

As for my verdict on Amy's mysterious death, I personally believe it was an accident brought on by illness. In 1956, Ian Aird, a professor of medicine at the Royal Postgraduate Medical School in London, proposed a compelling theory: that Amy's broken neck may have been the result of cancerous deposits in her spine—a condition common in advanced breast cancer. This would have left her bones extremely brittle, potentially fragile enough to fracture from even a minor fall.[88]

It should also be noted that Dudley was reportedly deeply shocked and bewildered upon learning of his wife's fatal fall—hardly the reaction one would expect from a murderer.

Dead but Awake

25.
THE WIND IN THE CEMETERY

In a book that's riddled with miserable stories, the following tale is right up there with the most tragic.

I first learned of this unfortunate episode during a conversation in late 2021 with Stuart Holloway, the manager of Oxford Walking Tours. We were discussing the many notable figures buried in Holywell Cemetery—among them the composer Sir John Stainer and the often-overlooked Inkling, Charles Williams.

Holywell Cemetery is next to St Cross church, not far from Magdalen College and just north of Long Wall Street.

Stuart told me about the legend of a headless ghost said to wander through the cemetery. When I began researching the story behind this eerie apparition, I uncovered one of the most tragic tales I've ever encountered. It was so profoundly sad that I was genuinely torn over whether to include it in this book.[89]

One thing I will say, in all sincerity, is that if *The Wind in the Willows* holds a special place in your heart, you may wish to consider skipping this chapter.

Kenneth Grahame, the most famous author buried in the cemetery, lies beside the grave of his son, Alistair Grahame.

Although born in Edinburgh, Kenneth Grahame was raised in Oxford, where he attended the prestigious St Edward's School. A bright and capable student, he deeply regretted never attending Oxford University—a dream his family couldn't afford to support. He did have a wealthy uncle, but unfortunately, the man refused to help.

Despite this setback, Grahame went on to enjoy a successful career in finance, eventually becoming Secretary of the Bank of England. Yet even with such a demanding role, he found time to write. In late 1908, he published his much-loved and brilliant critique of the old class system *The Wind in the Willows*.

Upon its publication, the book received a mixed response from critics, the literary critic for the *Evening Irish Times* wrote;

> "Mr Kenneth Grahame has written another book. This is an announcement of importance, for he is not a prolific writer, and most of us have many charming memories of *The Golden Age*. But *The Wind in the Willows* will puzzle people. Mr. Grahame's own publishers are themselves uncertain where to place it, for they describe it as "perhaps chiefly for youth" Average youth—of whichever sex—will not appreciate it, for they will take the book at its face value, and be mildly interested in the story of how the Mole became emancipated through his friendship with the Water Rat, and no more."[90]

Closer to home, the critic from *The Oxford Chronicle and Reading Gazette* had this to say...

> "This book is good in parts. In some parts it is very good, but the other parts sadly detract from that of the whole. Had Mr Grahame written two books—one a frankly Impossible children's tale, the other an idyllic nature story, he would have deserved praise, but to combine two incompatible things as he has done in *The Wind in the Willows* is to disappoint both sections of readers"[91]

Although history informs us that *The Wind in the*

Willows received a lukewarm reception upon its release, the book has certainly stood the test of time. It held deep personal significance for Kenneth Grahame, as the stories had originally begun as bedtime tales created to bring comfort and joy to his son, Alistair—who was born prematurely, was partially blind, and struggled with numerous health issues.

Although little Alastair was affectionately nicknamed 'Mouse,' he was, in fact, the inspiration for the character of Mr Toad. In terms of reckless behaviour, he certainly rivalled the exuberant amphibian. For mischief's sake, young Alastair would sometimes lie down in the road to stop cars, and while he was often bullied himself, he was also known for his violent temper, frequently lashing out at other boys in the schoolyard.

Many scholars believe that Mr Toad was Grahame's imaginative way of guiding his difficult son—using the character to gently teach lessons about responsibility and the importance of maturity. [92]

Off course, it's Mr Toad's long-suffering friends—Badger, Rat, and Mole—who are frequently forced to intervene whenever he indulges in his boy-racer fantasies, each of them reminding him to be 'a sensible Toad.' This mirrors the way the author often urged his own son to be 'a sensible Mouse'.

Alistair was severely bullied at both Rugby School and later at Eton. He suffered a nervous breakdown and was eventually withdrawn to be privately tutored in Surrey. Kenneth Grahame appeared to hold entirely unrealistic expectations for his son, using personal connections to secure Alistair a place at Christ Church. It all suggests a man determined to see his son achieve the Oxford education he had been denied himself—but one is left wondering: at what cost?

It was a fragile 'Mouse' that arrived at Christ Church

in 1918. Over the next few years he struggled, failing his scripture, Greek, and Latin exams three times. In 1919, his tutor ominously wrote 'Pass or go' beside his name in the college records, placing immense pressure on the troubled young man—another failure would mean expulsion.

On 7 May 1920, Mouse had just finished dinner in the Great Hall of Christ Church when, according to fellow student Thomas P.J. Beighton, he did something out of character: he asked the waiter for a glass of port and even invited Thomas to join him. Mouse was known to be quiet and reserved and had never been known to drink alcohol.

Later that night, he walked alone through the open fields of Port Meadow. Near an allotment, he lay down on the train tracks. At approximately 2:53 a.m., Inspector Ernest George Wootten received word that a tragic incident had occurred. Alastair Grahame had taken his own life—death by decapitation—just five days before his twentieth birthday. When his body was found, his pockets were stuffed with religious books he had been studying for his scripture exam.[93]

According to the newspapers, the jury at the coroner's court concluded that Mouse's death was accidental -attributed to his failing eyesight and being out late at night on a railway crossing. In truth, this was a cover-up, carried out of respect for the author, who never fully recovered from the loss of his only child and became a recluse. Twelve years later, he would be buried in a grave beside his son.

One positive change inspired by the tragedy of Mouse was Oxford University's first-ever legislation of special provisions for disabled students—an acknowledgment of his suffering.[94]

There was no wind blowing through the willows when I visited the cemetery to pay my respects to Kenneth and Mouse in the summer of 2025, and there was no sign of the authors headless son stumbling around the grave stones, there was however, an uncomfortable chill in the air which accompanied a pervading sense of sadness.

Paying my respects to Kenneth Grahame and Mouse
{Photograph} Kirk Ellingham

Dead but Awake

26.
MALICE IN THE PALACE

Blenheim Palace lies just six miles north of Oxford, set within 2,100 acres of parkland. It was the birthplace of Winston Churchill and is currently the residence of the 12th Duke of Marlborough.

The palace was originally built as a grand monument to military triumph, commemorating victory over the French in the War of the Spanish Succession. In recognition of his heroic leadership at the Battle of Blenheim in 1704, Queen Anne granted the estate to John Churchill, the 1st Duke of Marlborough.

On 15 April 2024, I visited Blenheim Palace to attend the popular Icons of British Fashion exhibition, which showcased designs by some of the most celebrated figures in British fashion, including Stella McCartney and Vivienne Westwood. During my visit, I struck up a conversation with one of the gallery assistants—Ramona, a long-standing tour guide—who told me all about the numerous ghosts said to haunt the palace, including a few she claimed to have seen herself.

Romana: "I recently saw what appeared to be the late duke {the eleventh}, pacing around the green drawing room, switching the lights off, which he often did to save energy.

I had to look twice but it definitely appeared to be him, his hair combed over to the side, wearing his check shirt, dark tie, green tweed jacket and tawny coloured trousers, his usual outfit.

It was around this time that the lead housekeeper Kate said that she often heard the alarms going off in a bedroom the late duke used to use, these alarms would often go off whilst we were conducting tours on his floor, the other strange occurrence was that the windows in his room kept being opened.

Kate asked the staff 'Who locked up and why didn't you shut the windows?'

One of the cleaners replied, 'I locked up, shut the windows and locked the doors'

After this happened for a third time, Kate cottoned on to the fact that there was something very strange and possibly supernatural happening in the duke's old bedroom.

And the duke was known to want plenty of fresh air in the palace, he had a saying, 'I'll have to have the bodies in, but I don't like the smell of them', by bodies he meant the visitors to the palace, not dead bodies!

So, the duke didn't mind people being around the palace as long as there was plenty of fresh air, he always kept the windows open.

Kate decided to address the late duke personally, she said, 'Your grace, this is quite enough, thank you' and this seemed to work, the windows no longer opened by themselves.

One day I had finished giving a tour when I saw one of the house keepers looking through a jumbled pile of worn-out pillows.

I asked her 'what are you going to do with all those pillows?'

She said 'I think the best thing is to have them thrown out on Monday'

When she came back into work on Monday morning, all the pillows had been smartly arranged, as though ready to be pillow cased, and all the old bed linen, which she had thrown on to the floor, looked as though it had been freshly pressed.

She asked all the house maids if they had touched the old pillows and they replied that they hadn't - we believe it simply must have been a ghost, perhaps the ghost of a maid who worked under the ninth duke.

According to legend, this poor maid was informed at the last minute that 100 guests were expected, which meant she had to prepare 100 bedrooms, she apparently went mad and ran around the palace screaming, two men carted her off to a psychiatric hospital, although no one knows what came of the maid, her screams and footsteps have been heard throughout the palace for years.

In 2015, we had the Untold Story exhibition at the palace which highlighted the stories behind the scenes of the resident family over the years.

One day, I was at the exhibition when I saw someone or something come in and out of the exit, I saw the persons shadow in the light, it was definitely the shadow of a bodily figure, this happened three times, I thought "who is joking around, going out and coming back in again"- when I checked there was no one in the vicinity."[95]

Ramona's stories are fascinating, but it turns out there's another spirit causing malice in the palace—this one is said to haunt the west wing.

On 12 July 2022, I interviewed a man we shall call Mr O, who spent his youth living with his family in the west wing of Blenheim Palace. His father was responsible for the horses and bred dogs for the 10th Duke of Marlborough and the Duchess. The family had moved to the palace from a farm in Chipping Campden, initially at the duke's request, due to his particular interest in Arab stallions.

The family's living quarters were spacious. Mr O recalled a thirty-foot-long passageway with rooms branching off on either side—the first being the lounge, followed by four large bedrooms. At the end of the passageway was the kitchen, where the family often gathered. Entry to the flat was through a solid oak door.

According to Mr O, the family would often hear the front door open and the latch drop, followed by the unmistakable sound of heavy footsteps moving along the passageway. However, the steps always stopped at the kitchen door. The sound frequently prompted the head of the family—who did not believe in ghosts—to put the kettle on, assuming one of the children had returned home early from school, only to find no physical presence in the passage. Over time, each member of the household was caught out by the phantom footsteps. The routine became so familiar that the family simply grew accustomed to it. In fact, Mr O told me:

"The footsteps didn't bother us. We thought, so what—let him or her trample down the passageway. They weren't doing us any harm."

Mr O also mentioned that there seemed to be no set time for the incident to occur and that no other strange things happened in any other section of their home. we may never uncover the identity of the invisible ghost with the heavy footwear, but Blenheim does seem to house a great number of ghosts, According to tradition, a man has been sighted on numerous occasions in the Dean Jones Room—almost always seen sitting in a chair, quietly reading a Bible. He is believed to be the Chaplain to the First Duke of Marlborough.

Another well-known manifestation at the Palace is said to be the ghost of a Roundhead soldier, reportedly seen either huddled by a fireplace or walking the corridors. This sighting aligns with the sound of footsteps often heard in the Stableman's flat. However, the timeline raises questions, as the Palace was built more than sixty years after the Civil War, although it could be the case that the soldier is perpetually re-treading his footsteps on land that the palace was built on, forever marching to the beat of a long-forgotten drum.[96]

27.
THE RESTLESS SPIRITS OF BLACKWELL'S BOOKSHOP

Blackwell's bookshop is an Oxford institution, the poet John Betjeman said he learned more in Blackwell's than in any of the libraries of Oxford. But the bookshop seemingly harbours a strange variety of ghosts.

Tucked away beside the shop's café is a hidden gem known as the Gaffer's Room—a beautifully preserved space that has served many purposes over the years. In the 1800s, it was the family's drawing room; later, it became the head office of Blackwell's (hence the room's name). In more recent times, it has been used as a quiet space for conducting interviews.

Benjamin and Basil Blackwell were known to be employers who cared about the welfare of their staff. this might be the reason why one of their employees has apparently never left. The ghost in question is said to be a maid dressed in Victorian uniform, believed to have worked for the Blackwell family. She is often seen in the offices above the Gaffer's Room, which once served as the family's sleeping quarters.

The most recent reported sighting occurred in the early 2000s. A long-serving employee looked up from her fax machine and saw the maid quietly wandering around the room before vanishing. Remarkably, she wasn't particularly alarmed; she claimed to have seen the maid on several occasions.

Meanwhile, beneath the lair of the phantom maid lies the Norrington Room, in the basement of Blackwell's. It proudly holds a place in the Guinness Book of Records as the bookshop space with the largest number of books in all of Europe.

Construction of the Norrington Room began in the mid-1960s. With five kilometres of shelving planned, a large team of carpenters was brought in for the job. In the early stages, the men worked in a pit of darkness, with working burners to light their way.

According to one account, a carpenter said he saw something so terrifying that he refused to return to the site. He told the foreman, in all seriousness, that he had looked up from his work and saw a dancing bear on what is now the landing.

When the Norrington Room was finally completed, two full-time carpenters remained on-site for a while to complete the finer details of the shelving. Thankfully, neither of them encountered the infamous dancing bear.

I searched through old newspaper archives but couldn't find any specific reports of dancing bears on the Blackwell's side of Broad Street. However, dancing bears were a common sight in Oxfordshire until the mid-1800s, and bear baiting is known to have taken place at the King's Arms pub—just a stone's throw from the bookshop.

Of course, the bears weren't dancing out of joy. These poor creatures were forced to place their front paws onto sheets of hot iron, causing them to rear up in pain. They were then beaten with sticks to make them "dance." Their existence was one of cruelty and misery.

The third ghost said to haunt Blackwell's Bookshop hasn't been seen inside the building, but on top of it. In 2011, the shop's neighbour, the New Bodleian Library, began an extensive renovation to transform the space into a state-of-the-art archival facility. The result of that ambitious project is now known as the Weston Library.

One morning, not long after the construction work had begun, security staff at the Bodleian contacted Blackwell's with an unusual question: had anyone been in the shop around 4:30 a.m.—or, more specifically, on the roof?

Blackwell's responded that no one had been in the building at that hour; in fact, the earliest anyone could access the shop was 7 a.m.

Yet the Bodleian Library's security cameras had captured something strange: a figure, draped in what appeared to be a white shroud, standing on the roof of the bookshop at around 4:30 a.m. When the footage was reviewed, no one could identify the figure clearly. It appeared human in shape, entirely dressed in white, and was seen standing silently, facing the graduation hall across the street. Moments later, it vanished behind a chimney.

Who—or what—it was remains a mystery.

A Victorian maid, a dancing bear, and a white spectral figure certainly make for an unusual cast of ghosts—but the ground on which Blackwell's stands hasn't always been the genteel, book-lined haven we see today.

Behind the original shop, near where the Norrington Room now lies, there once ran a narrow alley called Bliss Court. More a passageway than a proper street, it was home to a largely forgotten community of "fallen" women, alcoholics, and the destitute, people with hard lives and difficult stories, Benjamin Blackwell remembered it as anything but "blissful".[97]

When Benjamin Blackwell first opened his bookshop on this neglected side of Broad Street, some disapproved. The more refined booksellers had established themselves on the opposite side of the street, closer to the heart of the city. But those rival shops are now little more than fading memories. like the dancing bears and Victorian maids—long gone, while Blackwell's endures.

Dead but Awake

28.
THE GHOSTS OF WYTHAM WOODS

On Wednesday 28 February 2024, *Days of Chivalry*, a romantic medieval fantasy made in Oxford had its world premiere at the Phoenix Picturehouse on Walton Street, celebrated music producer Sebastian Reynolds had composed and recorded an evocative soundtrack for the movie and a full house attended the screening.

Sadly, none of the actors managed to attend the screening, they were all dead, the film was made in 1924, it had taken just over a century for it to make its cinematic debut.

Apart from a few scenes filmed in Scotney castle, *Days of Chivalry* was shot on location in Wytham Woods, a 423.8-hectare mixed deciduous forest of great scientific importance, where pioneering ecological studies have taken place for years. It is regarded as the most studied woodland in the world.

The unearthing of the film came about after a chance meeting between Sebastian Reynolds and Nigel Fisher, the Conservator of Wytham Woods.

The film, a significant landmark in early cinema, was directed by Hazel Ffennel, an accomplished musician, artist, and producer of plays who made several amateur movies between 1924 and the mid-1930s, most of which have long disappeared.

The ambitious film features dozens of extras and horses, Ffennel herself took on a small role as a goat-herder. Clocking in at 90 minutes, the film is pretty long for a movie of its time, especially as it was produced by a single individual, not a large conglomerate studio, which would have been the norm for a project of this scope, it's also worth noting that she was a female film maker in an industry dominated by men.

Hazel Ffennel however, had the finances to chase her dreams, her father was Colonel Raymond William Ffennell, a wealthy South African gold-mining pioneer who owned the estate of Wytham Woods

Sadly, Hazel's life was cut short in her thirties, the cause of her death was a brain tumour.

Colonel Ffennel and his wife Hope bequeathed the entire Wytham Woods to the university of Oxford in memory of Hazel, this was the biggest gift the university had received since the medieval times.

It is therefore only fitting that the land is also known as the Woods of Hazel, and according to the University of Oxford's official information pamphlet on Wytham, Hazel's ghost has been seen, jauntily running along the hillside of the estate, still enjoying the woodland she loved so much prior to her untimely death in 1939.

But Hazel is not the only ghost said to haunt Wytham Woods.

Some years ago, in the early 1990s, a Wytham resident was walking along the road from the Woods to the village with her boyfriend, when they encountered a hooded figure heading the other way who wished them a good evening; it was only as the figure passed them that they noticed it was floating several inches above the ground. The figure continued to float down the road until it vanished off towards the Walled Garden. Nigel, the conservator of Wytham Woods knew the couple and especially the woman's family. He described them to me as level-headed and down-to-earth.[98]

In medieval times, many pilgrims made their way from Cirencester to Canterbury via Wytham woods, perhaps the floating monk is one such pilgrim, hoping that one day he will actually make it to Canterbury cathedral.

Going back to the grand cinematic debut of *Days of Chivalry*, Hazel had only shown her films to enchanted villagers in local barns, now it was being screened to over 200 sophisticated auteurs in a crammed auditorium, the manual cranking of a projector wheel was off course now replaced by the single pressing of a button, an atmospheric soundscape supplanting the silence, what would Hazel have made of all this, well she was clearly a pioneer of her time, .. I think she would have loved it!

Hazel seems to be one of more cheerful ghosts to have appeared within the pages of this book, the same cannot be said for the ghosts which haunt the building directly next door to the Phoenix picture house, The Jericho Tavern.

Dead but Awake

29.
THE JERICHO TAVERN POLTERGEISTS

The Jericho Tavern is a well-established music venue in Oxford, many famous bands have rocked its stage over the years including Supergrass and Radiohead, who famously signed a record contract at the Jericho after playing what was only their eighth gig.

But it's been reported that when the amps are switched off and the punters have gone home, things start to get a little bit weird in the Tavern.

Asher Dust conjuring up some musical magic at the Jericho Tavern.
{Photograph} Tom McDonnell

In 2025, a sound engineer told me that he witnessed wine glasses, which were placed upon a drying rail, fly dramatically through the air, a live in chef who has long moved out, claimed that he often heard footsteps going up and down the staircase accompanied by children's laughter.[99]

There is a rumour that the Tavern, which dates to 1815, operated as a psychiatric hospital for children in the Victorian times, I have found no such evidence, there had been a previous building on the same site called The Jericho House built around 1650, which served as an inn for travellers seeking shelter after the city gates had closed.

Jericho is an affluent, highly sought after neighbourhood to live, this hasn't always been the case. Reports from the 1800s inform us that early homes in Jericho were built with very poor drainage. Low-lying land and a lack of basic drainage in these homes would result in flooding which, alongside open sewers and overcrowding, resulted in deaths from diseases such as dysentery and typhoid, there were twenty-two cases of cholera in 1832 and five typhoid deaths in 1872.

Poor Arthur Higgins, the son of the innkeeper, died at the age of four in Jericho House on 27 January 1865, it is perhaps not surprising, given the squalid conditions that the locals faced, that the Jericho Tavern seemingly harbours some very disgruntled ghosts.

30.
GHOSTS IN THE KITCHEN, THIEVES IN THE PANTRY

St Clare's is a private school for students aged 15 to 19, specialising in the International Baccalaureate Diploma. Located in leafy North Oxford, the school is spread across several nearby streets, combining grand Victorian red-brick houses with Edwardian buildings. Founded in the early 1950s, St Clare's grew out of an initiative to foster connections between British and European students in the years following the Second World War.

135 Banbury Road is a large Victorian mansion, once a dwelling- it is now one of St Clare's buildings and until the early 2020s, it housed the school's kitchen.

According to Jordon, one of the long-serving chefs, staff locking up the old kitchen sometimes felt as though they were being watched through the servery hatch that connected the dining area to the kitchen. There were also frequent reports of phantom footsteps echoing through the space, Jordon also told me that "there were instances where the door would slam behind you as if someone had been following you and purposefully slammed it".[100]

It seems that we've established that the paranormal entity at 135 Banbury Road likes to hang around the kitchen and the dining hall. Fittingly, when I dug into the British Newspaper Archives, I found that most of the stories linked to the house also revolved around food.

During the Great War, a Belgian lady living at the house, Madame Teels, made a heart-warming appeal. Eager to "do her bit" for the war effort, she sought a plot of land where she could grow potatoes to help with food production.[101]

Eight years earlier in 1909, *The Oxford Chronicle*

and Reading Gazette published a very different story concerning the house.

It was three days prior to New Year's Eve- 1909, when thieves broke into the mansion and stole food from the pantry, enough food was stolen for the story to make the local newspaper, the offenders were never caught, it was hardly the crime of the century but it was certainly a crime of its era.[102]

But why did the thieves only steal food? Why didn't they nab the family silver or nick a painting or two.

I personally think that this crime reeks of an inside job—or at least a tip-off from someone on the inside. The mansion is gigantic, but the thieves managed to find the kitchen in the middle of the night and slipped away unnoticed before the household realised. Perhaps a shady butler whispered word of a feast to his dodgy cousin, or maybe a local rogue overheard a butcher bragging about the giant goose destined for the New Year's banquet.

I asked a police sergeant for his professional opinion, and he agreed that it was highly likely that the thieves had some inside knowledge.[103]

As for why the thieves only stole food, another police officer speculated, "Maybe the burglars were discerning, and the silverware was junk".[104]

A criminal sociologist came up with some interesting theories, one which suggested that the thieves were testing to see how easy it was to get into the mansion with the intended aim of breaking in later on to steal more expensive items.[105]

The chef at St Clare's had mentioned that people felt as though they were being watched through the servery hatch, I asked him whether a person could actually fit inside the servery hatch, he laughed at first—but then admitted that it would be quite possible. The hatch, after all, was about the size of a double window. [106]

We know what caused the bumps in the night at the mansion three days before the new year in 1909. But could it be that the same rogues are still bumping around the house now —or is the unseen presence sensed by the staff the spirit of a former employee, still keeping watch against intruders? We may never know—but it's certainly been fun to hazard a guess.

Before we close this chapter, I must mention a conversation I had in September 2025 with a gentleman we'll call Jay, who once lived at St Clare's College. When I brought up the ghostly rumours, he didn't so much as blink. He told me he had often heard things go bump in the night—sounds he could never explain—and had even seen the tassels on lampshades stir in a breeze that simply wasn't there.

Dead but Awake

31.
OLD GHOSTS IN THE NEW THEATRE

There has been a theatre on George Street since 1836. Its first incarnation was the 'Vic,' named after Queen Victoria. In the 1880s, it was rebranded as the New Theatre, and the current building opened in 1934, boasting a spectacular revolving stage. In 1977, the name changed again to the Apollo until 2003, when it was once more rebranded as the New Theatre, presumably to keep the local taxi drivers confused.

In the early 1990s, Nuala Young and Eva Wagner, members of the Oxford Guild of Guides, gathered a collection of eerie stories surrounding the Theatre.

They came across reports of cloudy blobs that had mysteriously appeared in early photographs of the theatre from the 1880s. They also learned that in the 1970s, frightened workmen reported feeling as though they were being watched while carrying out repairs. The workmen also claimed that electrical tools were mysteriously unplugged, objects inexplicably moved, and cables spliced without explanation.[107]

We can't be certain of the identity of the New Theatre poltergeist, but I recall a conversation from many years before I began research for this book. A lady told me that her father had worked at the New Theatre in the 1980s and believed the place was haunted. From what I remember, his experiences closely mirrored those of the workmen from the seventies, particularly stories of objects mysteriously moving on their own.

I'm afraid the only story that I know of anyone being horrified at the New Theatre took place after a David Bowie performance in the 1970s, Walter, a former colleague of mine, was on duty outside the dressing room when a massive bouquet of flowers from an admirer arrived.

"Oh, thank you—they're beautiful," said Bowie, his face lighting up as he stretched out his arms to receive the flowers. But as the courier walked past him, he said, "They're not for you, sir. They're for Mick Ronson"... Bowie's guitarist.

Bowie apparently froze with his arms still outstretched, paralysed … by the horror of embarrassment.[108]

32.
THE HAUNTING OF A TRAUMATISED MIND

This is the only chapter of this book which investigates an account which is admittedly, likely to be non-supernatural, and may go some way to strengthening a sceptics stance on the paranormal, for it offers a logical alternative to what could be interpreted by some as an encounter with the paranormal.

When my friend Eva Wagner taught German at Brasenose College, one of the men in charge was a retired policeman who was a very strict and severe individual.

Despite his cold demeanour, he once confided in Eva that, as a young policeman fresh on the beat in Oxford, he had a haunting experience. One evening, he entered Radcliffe Square and spotted a student climbing the Radcliffe Camera—a grand, 140-foot-tall, 17th-century reading room of the university library. The officer chose to remain silent, planning to arrest the student once he came back down. Tragically, the plan became irrelevant when the student slipped and fell to his death.

The policeman told Eva that the event haunted him for the rest of his life. Each time he passed the Radcliffe Camera, he claimed to see the student fall. This chilling vision- part memory, part hallucination, repeated itself for years after the young man's death.[109]

Upon hearing this account, I began to wonder whether a traumatic experience, like the one endured by the policeman, could compel someone to believe they've seen a ghost, when in reality, they may be witnessing nothing more than a figment born from the depths of a traumatised mind. This theory could potentially explain a large number of 'sightings'.

Evening in Radcliffe Square
By Gus Mills

Alternatively, from a believer's perspective, it could be argued that a traumatic experience might heighten a person's awareness of paranormal phenomena. Could a close encounter with death, by default, tune a person's mind closer to the frequency of the afterlife?

The first theory, one a sceptic would likely support, certainly invites contemplation and scrutiny. However, I readily admit that a psychiatrist specialising in post-traumatic stress disorder would be far better qualified than I am to explore this area.

Less than a week after Eva told me about the policemen's incident, by sheer coincidence, a chap named Mark, a retired college porter, regaled an insightful follow up story to the fallen scholar's death, a first-hand account which was told to him when he accidentally gate-crashed a reunion of former Oxford students at the Turf Tavern, in the late 1990's..

Mark had stumbled into conversation with a group of ageing alumni of Exeter and Trinity college, he discovered that the student who fell to his death, died not long after World War 2, at a time when students would sleep two to a room and four would attend a tutorial, to try and make up for years lost in war.

The man who climbed the Radcliffe Camera was at the time a student at Lincoln college, he hadn't clambered to the roof for a prank, as I had assumed, but was attempting to fix the lightning conductor on the top of the Radcliffe Camera, which he noticed had sprung free, he apparently had climbed most of the way up before he fell, broke his back and died, the very next day, two students from Lincoln's main rival, Exeter college, climbed to the top of the Rad Cam and fixed the lightning conductor themselves, in the name of college one upmanship, to prove that they could put it right without killing themselves, and also in memory of the chap who had died.

One of the old boys in the Turf told Mark, "It might seem really callous now, but we had seen so much death in the war that one more death didn't really make a difference, and part of us missed the excitement and adrenaline of the war".

Mark reminded me that the student reunion at the Turf was comprised of the same generation of post war adrenalin junkies who would race in either motorbikes or sports cars, from Carfax in the centre of Oxford to Piccadilly Circus, wealthy students who could afford Vincent cars, powerful vehicles which the police couldn't possibly catch in their inferior automobiles.

The former soldier-students from Exeter college, who had fixed the lightning conductor, had seemingly developed a blunt resilience to trauma, in contrast to the poor policeman who found himself perpetually haunted by a ghostly vision of regret, which we assume was all in his mind... or was it?[110]

33.
DISHWASHING MARY

On 2 February 2023, I attended a pre-lunch tour of Oriel College, organised by the college's Development Officer. During the visit, I was shown around the dining hall, which had recently undergone some minor renovations. While we were there, a few staff members shared a curious piece of college folklore—a resident ghost affectionately named Mary by past employees.

Mary is most often seen standing in the doorway that leads to the kitchen, quietly cleaning a dish with a cloth. Her apparition, they told me, has been regularly spotted over the decades, suggesting that her presence has become something of a familiar fixture within the college.

In early 2024, Ghost story enthusiast Iain Stevenson provided me with some more information regarding sightings of Mary. In 2022, Iain was taking some visitors on a tour of Oriel when he felt compelled to ask the night porter if the college had any ghosts, to which he replied "Oh yes we have a ghost in the kitchen", the story goes that all three of the night porters have individually seen Mary in the exact same location.

There is a staircase underneath the dining hall which leads to a long corridor which the porters walk along as part of their night patrol duties, all three night porters claim to have seen a woman stood by one of the doors which leads to the kitchen area, they say that she wears what appears to be a Victorian dark pinafore and she is always seen polishing a plate and looking ahead, when the porters do a double-take the maid is said to suddenly disappear, each of the night porters initially didn't mention to anyone that they had seen a ghost, it was only by chance conversation that they realised they had all seen the same thing, It seems that Mary is not her official name, but a name which the night porters have given her.[111]

It is said that Mary's features are difficult to make out, as she appears more like a silhouette than a fully formed figure. One legend that has circulated suggests she took her own life after being jilted at the altar—though there is no evidence to support this theory. Regardless of the truth behind her story, it seems clear that Mary has been dealt a sorrowful fate, doomed to spend eternity quietly washing dishes in the shadows.

34.
THE CASTLE AND THE PRISON

At the turn of the twenty-first century, the remnants of Oxford Castle and Prison were reborn as a plush hotel and a thriving tourist attraction. But beneath its polished veneer lies a past steeped in legend and soaked in blood. The castle's foundations were laid in 1071 by the French master mason Robert D'Oyly, just five years after he arrived in England alongside William the Conqueror during the Norman invasion. At the time, the imposing structure would have dominated the western skyline of Oxford. Saint George's Chapel, now lost to history, once served as the castle's place of worship. Today, only the crypt remains, an ancient, atmospheric chamber carved from stone over nine centuries ago. The crypt is arguably the oldest seat of learning in Oxford, and quite possibly the oldest in all of England.

It is little wonder that the castle is believed to be haunted, it has been a site of many conflicts, its history immersed in many of the legendary battles of England.

The twelfth-century War of the Anarchy saw two of William the Conqueror's grandchildren, King Stephen and Empress Matilda, locked in a brutal struggle for the English throne. These warring cousins waged a bloody campaign of sieges and skirmishes across the realm.

In 1142, Empress Matilda found herself trapped in Oxford Castle, besieged by Stephen's forces. After three months of confinement, she made a daring and now-legendary escape. According to tradition, it was a snowy December day when Matilda slipped away from the castle tower with three of her knights. To avoid detection, the group disguised themselves in white cloaks to blend into the snow. in something reminiscent of a classic fairy tale,

Matilda wore a white fur coat.

In what could be described as one of the most spectacular escape stories in history, she reportedly passed unnoticed through enemy lines and skated across the frozen River Thames to the safety of Wallingford Castle.[112]

Five hundred years later, when Cromwell's troops forced the Royalist occupiers of Oxford to surrender, the Parliamentarians significantly strengthened the castle's fortifications. The upgrades were so effective that from the 17th century until as recently as 1996, the castle served as Oxford's official prison.

Chapter 39 delves into one of the most high-profile public executions to have taken place in the Castle courtyard, one of many to have been held there, In the early stages of his career, the castle courtyard served as the workplace of Jack Ketch, arguably the most notorious executioner in British history. For those unfamiliar with his story, Ketch's infamy spread throughout London in the late 17th century after he botched a series of high-profile executions. Crowds of onlookers often fainted or vomited as he made clumsy swings with his axe, frequently missing the neck and striking other parts of the body. His carelessness prolonged the deaths of political prisoners such as the Duke of Monmouth. Debate persists as to whether his actions were the result of drunkenness or the deliberate cruelty of a sadist. Either way, his infamy was such that he served as the inspiration for The Hangman in the Punch and Judy shows.

The 17th-century biographer Anthony Wood provides us with some grim details of an execution carried out by Jack Ketch in the Oxford Castle courtyard at 11 a.m. on 31 August 1681. According to Wood's account, Ketch cut the rope of the gallows before the condemned man had died of strangulation. This, however, was not an act of mercy on Ketch's part—as Wood makes chillingly clear…

"Stephen College, born at Watford in Hertfordshire, nephew to Edmund College of St. Peter's in the Bayly, suffered death by hanging in the castle yard Oxon, and when he had hanged about half an hour was cut down by Catch or Ketch, and quartered, under the gallows, his entrails were burnt in a fire made by the gallows. He spoke and prayed more than half an hour, his body was, after quartering, put into a coffin, and the same day was conveyed to London, and buried privately the Thursday following at night in St. Gregory's church near St. Paul's."[113]

CASTLE AND PRISON IN PRESENT TIMES

The castle ceased functioning as a prison in 1996 after it was deemed unfit for purpose. Today, it stands as a popular tourist attraction. Some of the original cells remain unchanged since the prison's closure. I've stepped into one of them myself… a cramped, claustrophobic space measuring just 1.6m by 3.6m.

Given the castle's brutal history, it's no surprise that numerous ghost sightings have been reported over the years. In the late 1990s, tour guide Eva Wagner led ghost tours around the castle while it was in the process of being transformed into a tourist attraction. At the time, security was tight to prevent people from wandering into the area, which was undergoing large-scale renovations. Curious about a rumour she had heard, Eva asked one of the guards about another guard's reaction to having apparently seen a ghost. In her own words…

"I was wandering around the castle conducting a ghost tour in the late 1990s, security guards were also wandering around the premises, I chatted with one of the guards and mentioned that I had heard that one of his colleagues had been admitted to the Warneford, a psychiatric hospital, after he thought he'd seen something supernatural in the old prison, as I said this, another guard rushed by with a big Alsatian and shouted in a matter-of-fact way 'Oh yes he did see something,' half confirming the rumour but without explaining exactly what the guard had actually seen."

What kind of ghost could have driven a security guard to a psychiatric hospital? We may never know for certain, but in 2017, my friend Jordon Sha-Hembury witnessed something truly terrifying at the Oxford Castle and Prison.

Jordon, whom I met at a martial arts academy in 2019, is, like me, a lifelong enthusiast of all things paranormal. Since 2015, he has taken part in numerous investigations across the United Kingdom.

Jordon, back at the Oxford Castle, around a decade after helping with an interesting paranormal hunt.
{Photograph} Tom McDonnell

In 2017 he worked with a Nottingham-based team of ghost hunters who were conducting a paranormal investigation at Oxford Castle. Jordon was assisting-with equipment and refreshments for the investigators, many of whom had paid to take part in the hunt. In the early hours of the morning, one participant noticed his flashlight was missing and assumed he had left it upstairs near the old prison cells in D-Wing. Jordon volunteered to retrieve the flashlight.

This occurred around 3 a.m., a time when all guests had been instructed to remain in the base room. As Jordon reached the top of the stairs and retrieved the flashlight, he suddenly realised he wasn't alone. He clearly saw someone cautiously peering out from one of the cells, someone who seemed intent on not being seen. Naturally, Jordon assumed it was a mischievous guest who had broken the rules to sneak off and hide. To quote Jordon

"I was 100 percent certain there was a guest up there, in the cell, messing around".

Jordon called out loudly to the figure in the cell, reminding them that guests weren't allowed to wander the castle alone. When there was no response, his frustration grew. He marched into the cell, ready to confront the rule-breaker—only to receive the shock of his life: the cell was completely empty.

When Jordon reported the sighting to the rest of the investigative team, they barely batted an eyelid—such was their extensive experience with incidents like these.

No one seems to know the identity of this particular ghost—a mysterious figure doomed to linger eternally behind bars, haunting a squalid room adjacent to a padded cell.[114]

I must mention that this frightening incident did little to derail Jordon's enthusiasm for paranormal investigations, in-fact quite the opposite, he's still out there, tearing down the cobwebs and marching straight into the darkness, there's hundreds of others like him across the UK, nocturnal investigators of the supernatural, most un-blinkered in their determination to seek out a light of truth in a realm of shadows, and just before I sent *Dead but Awake* off to the printers, lo and behold, I met another ghost hunter, Angela. Not only had she attended the very same ghost hunt as Jordan, but she too had experienced paranormal activity there.

Angela's encounters with the castle's ghosts were more physical than Jordan's, beginning in the Debtors' Tower and continuing later in the crypt.

"It was the spirit of one of the prison guards, I could feel him pressing himself upon me. We were in a group that had climbed the stairs in the Debtors' Tower and were standing there, listening to the stories. Suddenly, I felt something pressing into me. There was a sense of malevolence… a certain kind of grubbiness.

It wouldn't stop. I moved to another spot in the room to shake it off, but it followed me and pressed into me again. I moved a second time, and again it followed. That's when I turned to my husband and said, 'There's something pushing at me.'

We eventually moved on into the area with the padded cells, and whatever it was stayed behind, in the Debtors' Tower.

Later, when we entered the crypt, I felt the presence of another spirit, a hooded monk who also seemed to press himself upon me. A woman standing nearby laughed nervously and remarked that I was being shadowed by a tall figure in a monk's hood.

We eventually sat in the cells within the crypt, but nothing more occurred. We did hear a few noises, though we chalked most of them up to my husband's grumbling stomach!"

It seemed that neither the prison officer nor the tall monk had any qualms about invading Angela's personal space. I began to wonder if, somehow, she had drawn them to her. As she went on to explain, Angela appears to be one of those people with a heightened sensitivity to the restless dead…

"In my previous home in Brize Norton, the figure of an old man was often seen at the bottom of the stairs. Both my husband and I are sensitive to spirits, and we were well aware of his presence. Even our old springer spaniel would frequently stare toward that spot on the stairs—where the faint outline of the figure could sometimes be seen." [115]

Jordon and Angela's reports are fascinating in their own right, but the following account from Amanda Goodger is one of the strangest I have ever encountered.

I met Amanda in 2024 when she attended a literary tour I was leading around Oxford. Afterward, she joined the group for a drink, and the conversation naturally turned to one of my favourite topics—ghosts. Amanda shared that she had witnessed something very strange at Oxford Castle back in the noughties.

We agreed to meet again to discuss that experience in greater detail. Then, by complete chance, I reached out to Amanda on a Friday the 13th in 2025, to arrange a follow-up meeting. At the exact moment Amanda received my WhatsApp message, she was walking into Oxford Castle for a paranormal hunt—only the second time she had attended one there. The first had been decades earlier, but it's Amanda's first excursion to the castle that we now turn to, her epic story however, begins in Evesham.

Amanda's First Trip to the Castle.

In the cosy confines of what is arguably Oxford's most haunted pub, The Trout, Amanda shared the following account.

"In the noughties, I lived in Worcestershire and worked for a government department based nearby. At the time, I was part of an informal paranormal group, and someone suggested we visit Oxford Castle—a place I had never been to before.

Before that trip, I attended a meeting of a Spiritual circle based in Evesham. The group met at a bookshop on Evesham High Street called Spiritus, which was run by a couple. The male owner was a particularly intriguing character—he had a distinctly Dickensian look and claimed that his guiding spirit was none other than John Dee, the legendary spiritual advisor to Queen Elizabeth I.

Many of the shops along Evesham High Street have medieval cellars—some dating back to the 13th century—and the bookshop was no exception. Its cellar, however, was particularly fascinating. It featured a blocked tunnel believed to lead to the nearby abbey.

Two days before the planned paranormal evening at Oxford Castle, I attended a separate paranormal event at the bookshop. We explored the entire building, including the basement. Down there, in the cellar, a circular table had been set up as part of the investigation

I was standing near where the entrance to the tunnel had once been. The tunnel itself had reportedly stretched about 200 yards, reaching close to the abbey on the other side of the road—though I didn't know that at the time. As I stood there, I noticed something unusual: my hands were positioned as if I were holding a book. At the same moment, I felt a distinct presence just to my right. I heard someone speaking to me in Latin, it was a strange, vivid sensation. That's when someone told me about the tunnel leading to the abbey.

In 1265, during the Battle of Evesham, Prince Edward (later Edward I) defeated the rebel forces. As the rebels fled through the High Street, many were cut down—some even tried to escape by forcing their way into nearby buildings. It's said that spirits from that bloody battle still haunt the area.

However, the man I saw—dressed entirely in black—didn't seem to be one of those restless soldiers. Still, he appeared to belong to that same era.

Two days after the investigation in the bookshop was my first visit to Oxford Castle. Before heading to Oxford, I returned to the bookshop to catch up with my friend who worked there. Toward the end of the day, a woman and her young daughter came in. I didn't recognise them.

The mother explained that she was struggling to cope with her daughter, describing her as "over-intelligent"- so much so that even the school didn't know how to handle her. While my friend spoke with the somewhat tense and overwhelmed mother, I chatted with the daughter.

I gently asked if she had an invisible friend. She said "yes".

Then, quite suddenly, she seemed to tune in to the energy of the shop. She pointed out something about the stairs, saying she felt that something bad had happened there. What she didn't know was that a woman had once hanged herself from a beam above that very spot.

The girl then mentioned sensing another presence in the basement – "a nasty man," she called him. She described him as a Victorian man wearing a top hat and a long dark mourning coat. There was a mannequin in the basement, but it was dressed as a monk, not like the figure she described.

Children that age don't usually make up things with such detail-especially not things they shouldn't reasonably know. In fact, the way she spoke felt more like talking to a teenager than a five-year-old.

I got the sense her mother wasn't comfortable with her talking this way. But everything the girl mentioned aligned eerily well with what I already knew about the shop. It confirmed, for me, that the place held a great deal of residual energy.

I turned to the mother and said, carefully, "I'm not sure whether to mention this, but… have you ever looked into alternative ways of understanding children like yours?"

The mother seemed curious, so I explained that some children are thought to have certain energetic traits—often referred to as Indigo, Crystal, or Rainbow children—linked to when they're born. I looked at the little girl and said, "I think your daughter might be a Rainbow."

The mother asked, "Is that a problem?"

I replied, "No, not at all. But the world she has to navigate might see it as one. I get the sense that's what you're reacting to—you're not just scared for yourself; you're scared for her too."

The mother asked, "How can I help her live in the world we all have to live in?"

I replied, "I don't really work with that side of things—but my friend does have some contacts who might be able to help."

My friend, who had been quietly listening, added, "Yes, I can put you in touch with some people if you're open to exploring that. I added "by the way—she's a gifted child."

The mother looked surprised. "Oh… you can see that?"

Oh yes", the friend nodded. "She's clearly gifted. But please remember—she also needs to stay grounded. It's important she has friends her own age and a connection to everyday life."

The mother then brought up her daughter's invisible friend.

I responded, "No, I'm not talking about imaginary friends. I mean the real world—the one we all live in. Keep her grounded, but don't dismiss the things that frighten you. Because those things are part of who she is. The key is to manage it carefully—so that people don't label her as strange, especially at her age."

I never stayed in touch. It was a one-off encounter. But it showed me something important: when children find themselves tuned into this kind of space, it needs to be managed carefully —especially while they're still young.

A little later, my friend closed the shop for the day. I was sitting by the till while she went downstairs. That's when it happened—a man began speaking to me in Latin. He appeared to be a high-ranking official, perhaps from the abbey. Then he made the sign of the cross above my head. It felt like a blessing, as if he were sending help with me for what lay ahead.

Moments later, my friend came back upstairs. I hadn't realised she was watching.

She looked at me and said, "What just happened? It looked like you were being blessed."

I replied, "Well, I didn't say anything…" She interrupted, "No—but I saw it. A cross—right above your head."

I nodded. "Yes. That's exactly what just happened."

After we wrapped up at the shop, my friend headed home, and I made my way to Oxford to meet a group of friends. There were seven of us in total. One of them had contacts at Oxford Castle, so this wasn't a formal or commercial event—it was more of an informal investigation. We weren't part of any official company; we were just a small group of friends with a shared interest in the paranormal.

We explored the castle grounds but didn't go into the old tower. We did, however, enter the prison and the cells. For me, the most intense moment came when we went downstairs into the crypt. The hairs on the back of my neck immediately stood on end. Right away, I thought, There's something down here.

This was before we even set up any equipment—we were just hanging around, having a look, as you do. But I got this overwhelming bad feeling that the energy was about to shift dramatically. Almost instinctively, I said, "Everyone needs to protect themselves. Do you know how to do that?"

One of the group asked, "What do you mean?"

I explained as best I could—though I'm no expert—that we needed to tune in and prepare ourselves because something urgent was coming. We didn't have a medium with us, just friends. I told everyone to visualize surrounding themselves with a white light—above, below, and all around—because something dark was about to descend.

Literally seconds later, it happened.

The presence that came in was unlike anything I'd ever felt before. The only way I can describe it is like the monster Grendel from Beowulf—an ancient, malevolent force meant to torment and terrorise. It felt like something incredibly old, something that existed long before the prison was built.

A black mist seemed to envelop us. It was genuinely terrifying. Very few things manage to shake me like this did.

I actually felt as though the blessing from the phantom clergyman back in Evesham had come to protect all of us in that moment. It was a situation where time seemed to lose meaning—what happened in the crypt lasted only about 30 seconds, but it was incredibly intense. Even after all these years, I remember the experience with startling clarity.

But the story isn't over. There's a twist.

Afterwards, three people brought their equipment downstairs. We had divining rods—two metal tubes that cross to indicate "yes" or "no"—along with a meter to measure energy levels and a temperature gauge, which showed the room getting extremely cold. It was clear something was there.

Using the divining rods, we began a sort of conversation with what turned out to be a priest's spirit.

Someone asked, "Did you come to Evesham with Amanda?"

The rods crossed: "Yes"

"Have you come with her tonight?"

Again, "Yes".

We asked for his name. "Is it Matthew?"

"No".

"Michael?"

"No".

I said, "I'm getting Peter."

The rods crossed again: "yes".

"Have you come here to protect us?"

No response.

"Have you come to protect somebody?"

"Yes."

Then we started naming people.

"Are you here to protect Amanda?"

"Yes"

"Are you here to protect her friends?"

"Yes"

So, this was the twist in the tale, because we had discovered that the priest from Evesham had protected us after we had felt the wrath of the malignant presence in the crypt."

Amanda's Second Trip to The Castle

Amanda enjoyed her second paranormal hunt at Oxford Castle, though she felt there was a little too much emphasis on the technology and not enough on the human experience. One memorable moment occurred during a session of table tipping in one of the old prison cells. Table tipping involves participants sitting around a table, resting their hands lightly on the surface, while the lead investigator invites any spirits present to move or tip the table as a sign of their presence.

This reminded Amanda of a much earlier encounter with table tipping—one that left a lasting impression. It took place many years ago at a paranormal event held in a 19th-century manor house called Craig-y-Nos, located in Abercrave, near the Swansea to Brecon Road in Wales. Though originally built for a sea captain, the house was purchased in 1878 by the renowned opera singer Adelina Patti—a wealthy and flamboyant figure who had an affair with Dante Gabriel Rossetti and even had her own opera house built onto the side of the estate.

During that earlier table tipping session, Amanda had an experience she would never forget. "Instead of tipping the table," she told me, "It felt like the spirit wanted to tip me over. I was shaken so violently I honestly thought my brain was going to rattle out of my head. I felt completely nauseous—physically ill. But as soon as I stepped out of the room, the feeling vanished."

It seemed, in that case, the spirit had tuned in not to the table, but to Amanda herself.

Back at the table tipping session in Oxford Castle, Amanda was naturally hesitant to get involved. "There were about six of us in the group," she said. "I didn't want to take part, and neither did my friend—we were both happy just to watch."

But Amanda had a strong feeling that, once again, it

wouldn't be the table that reacted—it would be her.

"To be honest, that's why I didn't want to sit at the table," she explained. "I wanted to be able to leave quickly if I needed to. I wasn't sure how the others would react if something happened again."

Sure enough, as soon as Amanda felt the familiar sensation building, she quietly left the room.

Later, the organiser asked Amanda if she'd like to try a Ouija board session in one of the other prison cells. Amanda agreed but asked if she could use a pendulum instead. It ended up being just Amanda, her friend, and one of the organisers.

After calibrating the pendulum, it seemed to work well for all three of them. The atmosphere was calm and focused, and the experience turned out to be quite positive. They kept it simple—just yes and no answers.

A young man came through first. He'd been imprisoned in the late 19th century for a minor offence. His energy felt light and innocent—he simply wanted to say hello. It was a warm, almost cheerful encounter, a stark contrast to the dark and terrifying experience Amanda had faced in the crypt years earlier.

A second presence seemed to appear toward the end— not as gentle, but not hostile either. Neutral, perhaps, but still clearly aware of their presence.

Amanda ended our conversation by saying, "My friend had to leave early—she had an appointment the next morning—so the rest of the group went down into the crypt. But this time, it felt like there was too much focus on the technology. Nothing really happened, and by that point, I was tired and ready to go home.

It wasn't a bad experience—I actually enjoyed it overall. But the thing that really spooked us… was your WhatsApp message. It came through just as we were walking into the castle!"[116]

35.
THE DIVINITY SCHOOL POT BOY

The pot boy has long held a place in the rich tapestry of English drinking culture. In the 1600s, he might be found hawking beer in the cobbled streets, shouting like a market trader, or dashing around a busy tavern working exhausting hours to serve drinks. By the era of Charles Dickens—who often mentioned pot boys in his novels—the role had evolved. Pot boys were now delivering beer from public houses directly to people's homes, offering a kind of Victorian-era twist on Deliveroo.

The toughest pot boys often served a dual purpose: not only delivering and serving beer but also acting as impromptu bouncers.

By the mid to late 19th century, however, the era of the pot boy was drawing to a close, largely due to two key developments. First came the Grocers' License Act of 1860, which permitted shops to sell alcohol for off-premises consumption. This is why we now refer to such shops as "off-licenses." The act significantly undercut the monopoly that pubs had on the carry-out trade.

The second blow came with the emergence of the barmaid. As the Reverend Charles Maurice observed in *Mystic London* (1875),

> "The discriminating visitor will decidedly prefer to receive his sandwich and glass of beer at the hands of a pretty barmaid rather than from an oleaginous potman in his shirt-sleeves"

The role of the pot boy all but disappeared with the outbreak of the First World War, as young men were called up to serve in the armed forces. With so many drawn into the conflict, few were left to fill such roles back home—

The Divinity School, the haunt of the limping pot boy.
{Photograph} Tom McDonnell

and the pot boy, already in decline, vanished entirely from the English pub scene.[117]

There is, however, one pot boy in Oxford who seems to have missed the memo about modern times. He is said to still serve ale in the magnificent 15th-century Divinity School. Originally built as a lecture hall and examination room for theology, this historic building is renowned for its stunning vaulted ceiling and grand door designed by Christopher Wren. It also serves as a plush antechamber where students gather to adjust their academic gowns before processing to the graduation hall.

The Divinity School pot boy probably hasn't poured ale for any recent graduates, and he certainly isn't listed in Oxford University's internal recruitment records, for tradition has it that he died during the construction of the Divinity school, sometime in the 1400s.

According to the research notes of Nuala Young and Eva Wagner, the young pot boy is said to walk into the Divinity School with a noticeable limp, perhaps bringing ale to workmen from a long-past era. Bodleian Library porters have reported seeing him enter the centre of the hall, only to vanish through the Wren doorway.

Legend has it that he was the son of one of the school's builders. A popular theory suggests that he was accidentally given too much strong beer, causing him to fall from the scaffolding to his death, explaining why the pot boy now limps as he wanders the halls. [118]

Over a few beers at a pub, I recently shared the sad tale of the Divinity School pot boy with some fellow ghost enthusiasts. We all agreed on one thing; wouldn't it be great if pot boys were still out there, serving beer on the streets of Oxford? Maybe the Oxford city council might consider reintroducing the concept…

Dead but Awake

36.
VIBES AND FREQUENCIES

In 2008, a good friend, Keith invited me and a couple of friends over to his home for a few drinks. At the time, Keith rented a property on Chatham Road in South Oxford. I have a vivid memory of the first time I walked into that house. It carried a strange, solemn atmosphere, as if the walls had once borne witness to some terrible event. To be fair, the dreary grey décor didn't exactly lift the atmosphere of the place, I later discovered that there may have been a paranormal twist behind the strange vibe I'd sensed in that house.

Before sharing the strange events of Chatham Road, I should mention that I may have inherited a somewhat heightened sense of awareness of such vibes, over the years, many relatives on my mother's side have claimed to possess the ability to detect paranormal energy, some of them genuinely believed that they could make contact with the dead.

When I was a child, a few of my relatives spoke so frequently about ghosts that the topic became a normal part of everyday conversation. In the mid-1980s, I was told of one sighting that I shall never forget.

My grandmother lived in a house in Belle Vale, Liverpool. One day, she claimed to have seen the apparition of a baby lying in a bed in the spare room. Startled, she ran from the room to tell her husband, who was initially sceptical of such stories. That was until he went to investigate and found a clear impression on the bed—as if a baby had just been lying there. After that, he never set foot in that room again.

Another strange incident connected to my grandmother- Cora Ellis, who passed away in 2010, occurred long after her death.

In June 2020, my grandnephew was just four years old and had obviously never met my grandmother, Cora. Yet, quite strangely, he began repeating her name over and over to his mother, something that puzzled everyone, as no one had ever told him about his great-grandmother or even mentioned her name. Later, when shown a family photograph taken in 1984 with eight people in it, including myself at around seven years old, he immediately pointed to my grandmother and said, "That's Cora. She's in space... she comes to see me." He then pointed to my late uncle, who passed away in 2001, adding, "He's in space too. He's a nice person."

The rest of the people in the photograph were still alive in 2001 and accordingly, 'not in space.' Incidentally, one of the relatives in this photograph is an aunt who once made her living as a medium and as a fortune teller, so clearly there seems to be a cross generational ability with-in the family to pick up on supernatural vibes.

Back to the house on Chatham Road, I couldn't help but tell Keith that I thought the vibe of his home had a somewhat sombre tone, Keith wholeheartedly agreed and said he was looking forward to moving out of the house, he also mentioned that on a number of occasions, a couple of friends had visited and stayed overnight, he said that one friend claimed to have fleetingly seen the shadowy figure of a woman stood on the second step from the top of the staircase. A few weeks after I had visited Keith's place, a mutual friend, Laura, spent a night in the spare room of the house after missing the last bus home.

The next day, by chance I bumped into Laura walking through the city centre of Oxford, she mentioned that she'd slept over at Keith's place and had seen his house mates in the early hours of the morning, two men who were stood in the kitchen, facing each other in silence,

Curious, I asked Laura to describe the men but she didn't get much of a chance to look at them, she said had to walk through the kitchen to use the bathroom and as she was a stranger, rambling around their home in the early hours, she felt a bit embarrassed so rushed straight past them, although she did notice that one of the men was middle aged with black curly hair, I couldn't bring myself to tell laura that Keith only had one house mate, and that was a woman who at the time was visiting relatives in Australia!.[119]

Convinced that something sinister had taken place at the house on Chatham Road, I launched an investigation. Hours slipped away at the Oxford History Centre, followed by even more digging through the British Newspaper Archives. Yet, despite my efforts, no reports of foul play surfaced. Still, I remain certain that the house conceals a dark secret of some sort.

My memories of the house on Chatham Road stirred something within me, prompting me to think about the vibes of different places, two questions lingered in my mind:

Firstly, why do some buildings seem to possess a definitive atmosphere?

Secondly, is it possible that the history of a building could somehow shape the vibe of the place?

These questions brought to mind an incident from 1996, when a German physicist named Matt was searching for a house to rent in East Oxford for himself and a few fellow students, including a mutual friend, Jake. Matt was instantly drawn to a house on Argyle Street. When the housing agent asked which room he preferred, Matt didn't hesitate—he pointed to one and said simply, "I like this room. It's got a good vibe.", Curiously, at that very moment, a wardrobe door creaked open on its own.

The agent was absolutely delighted to let the property

to Matt, especially since the property had sat vacant for nearly six years.

Matt would later discover that the house was the site of a notorious murder which had taken place only five years before he moved in.

On 13 April 1991, a nineteen-year-old student, Rachel McLean, accepted her boyfriend's marriage proposal, the very next day she was strangled to death by the same man, her body was hidden under the floorboards of the house, where it remained for seventeen days.

The murder took place in the very room Matt had singled out as having "good vibes" [120]

Evidently, the vibe of a house doesn't always reflect its history, or perhaps, it is more likely that only a select few possess a heightened sensitivity for such vibes.

In the summer of 2025, while interviewing Amanda Goodger about paranormal activity, our conversation turned to the subject of vibes and frequencies. Amanda had some fascinating views on the matter, and she told me…

"As human beings, we are like antennas. You have a nervous system. I have a nervous system. We all have endocrine systems. What many people don't realise is that these systems can respond to the natural environment in different ways from person to person. Take thunderstorms, for example—when the atmosphere becomes electrically charged, people often say the air feels "heavy" or "oppressive."

So why can't buildings—or places—carry similar charges? After all, all matter is still $E=mc^2$—energy and matter are interchangeable. So, when we talk about hauntings, in many ways, we're really talking about energy.

Throughout history, countless people have reported paranormal experiences. These stories have persisted across cultures and centuries. What connects all of this? One common thread: energy, and our ability to tune into it.

When we discuss hauntings or spiritual phenomena, we're often talking about people tuning in. Just like a television needs to be tuned to the right frequency, or a device connects to Wi-Fi through an invisible signal, our own systems might be picking up something—something real, though not always visible. A frequency. A form of energy."

In 2005, Amanda spoke with a shaman in Guatemala about her own experiences with the paranormal. He told her, "You need a proper teacher—you need to understand the frequencies you're dealing with."

Curious, Amanda asked, "What do you mean by frequencies?"

He explained that all humans operate on different frequencies. "Just look at EEG scans," he said. "It's science. The brain runs on electrical waves—alpha, beta, gamma, delta. When someone meditates, for example, they're often trying to reach the beta state—the calmest, quietest wave. It's all about tuning the brain."

"So once again, the idea of tuning in emerges—strong circumstantial evidence that we may, in fact, be tuning into different forms of energy, frequencies, or phenomena that not everyone is consciously aware of".[121]

37.
THE LORD OF THE SMOKE RINGS

Over the past few years, I've been gathering anecdotes about J.R.R. Tolkien from people who knew him as part of a project I'm working on. Although I've recently discovered that I may be able to go straight to the source. According to legend, Tolkien's ghost still haunts his last place of work: Merton College.

Tolkien with Pipe
By Jon Patterson

It has been claimed that Merton is one of the more academically rigorous Oxford colleges. It is the place, some say, where fun goes to die. Founded in 1264, its ancient buildings certainly wouldn't look out of place in Middle-earth.

Tolkien served as Merton Professor of English Language and Literature from 1945 until his retirement in 1959. People I've spoken to who knew him often recall the ever-present pipe in his mouth,[122] which makes it all the more fitting that his ghost is said to linger in his former study, where students have reported the unmistakable scent of pipe smoke...[123]

A perfectionist to a fault, Tolkien was known to endlessly revisit and revise the manuscripts of *The Lord of the Rings*, painstakingly reworking sentences and obsessing over the smallest details. When the book was finally completed, some of his colleagues believed he had squandered his time on a fantasy epic instead of focusing on the scholarly research he was paid to do.

Perhaps Tolkien is still at work in that study, pipe in hand, dreaming up new stories and reworking old ones, determined to perfect them, even in the afterlife.

38.
SLURPING PIGS

In Chapter 8, I focused on the ghosts of Pembroke College, based on my investigations from 2018. More recently, I discovered a 19th-century legend about a tavern called The Black Drummer Inn, which once stood just behind the college on Littlegate Street.

According to the legend, patrons of the Black Drummer Inn were regularly disturbed by a strange sound that seemed to permeate through the walls, a persistent, slurping noise unmistakably like that of a pig. Yet no such animal was ever found on or near the premises. One can only imagine the frustration of the landlord, trying to maintain a welcoming atmosphere amid such an eerie and inexplicable disturbance.

To solve the problem of this mysterious noise, the locals sent for the wise man of Abingdon, a market town five miles south of Oxford. The sage advised them to inspect the crypt of a neighbouring church, presumably St Aldate's, which still stands in the square but has undergone significant renovation since the 1800s.

Heeding the wise man's advice, the locals explored the crypt and, lo and behold, made a remarkable discovery: the uncorrupted body of a young man, perfectly preserved.

The wise man instructed the group to burn the body for no less than 24 hours. Yet, when the ashes were examined, the body appeared completely untouched by the flames. As a last resort, they turned to academics at the university, who recommended dismembering the body before attempting to burn it again. This time, the advice proved effective and sure enough, the strange slurping noise ceased.[124]

The Black Drummer Inn was torn down years ago.

Apparently, the last landlord—Henry Hogg, a rather fitting name given the pig theme—went bankrupt in 1871.[125]

There is a strange story about another long forgotten pub, The Red Lion Inn, which once stood in front of Pembroke college and St Aldate's church, at 4 Pembroke Street, the Red Lion Inn was mysteriously engulfed in flames on a bitterly cold night in the early hours of Friday, 24 March, 1899.

Fortunately, no one was injured in the blaze, thanks to the heroic efforts of the local firefighters who worked tirelessly to stop the flames from spreading to nearby buildings. Curiously, however, the cause of the fire could never be determined.

When a reporter from the local paper inspected the scene after the fire, he made no mention of uncorrupted corpses or eerie slurping sounds. He did, however, note one bizarre detail about the blaze, an observation that seems to defy all logic.

"The apartment presented a peculiar spectacle, later on Friday morning, when our representative visited the scene, the bottles being cracked and broken, as well as a large number of glasses and tumblers, the contents and furniture of the room were burnt beyond recognition, but it is somewhat strange that the ceiling has not fallen through, except in one corner, where it is supposed the fire first penetrated".

According to the report, and against all odds, the ceiling of the tavern had mysteriously withstood the flames, just like the uncorrupted body of the young man found in the nearby crypt a few centuries earlier.[126]

39.
BLESSED GEORGE

North Oxford's leafy Banbury Road is known for its rows of grand Victorian mansions, lining a stretch of just over six kilometres. But beneath its picturesque charm lies a darker tale: the road is said to be haunted by a headless ghost, believed to be the spectre of George Napier—or Napper, depending on the source.

A quick internet search on George Napier will turn up a surprising amount of misinformation. He is frequently—and wrongly—described as a highwayman, a myth perpetuated by high profile media outlets, tour companies, and even hoteliers. It's a lazy assumption, likely born from the fact that Banbury Road was once a hotspot for highwaymen and, admittedly, it makes for a good story. However, with just a little more effort, it becomes clear that George Napier was not a highwayman, but a holy man, venerated by Catholics. In fact, his legacy was formally honoured in 1962 with the founding of the Blessed George Napier Roman Catholic School in the market town of Banbury, some thirty miles north of Oxford. I could be mistaken, but I'm not aware of any primary schools named after musket-wielding murderers on horseback.

George Napier was born in Oxford in 1550, just five years before the death of Mary I, England's last Catholic monarch. With the coronation of Elizabeth I, the country swiftly became a dangerous place for practising Catholics. Almost immediately, a flurry of anti-Catholic legislation was introduced, casting followers of the "old faith" as enemies of the state.

For Catholics living under Elizabethan—and later Jacobean—rule, life became a perilous journey marked by suspicion and persecution. Napier's own path was no exception. At the age of twenty, after two years at Corpus Christi College, he was expelled for being a recusant. It was the first of many tribulations he would endure in a life defined by faith and resistance.

Forty years after his expulsion from Corpus Christi, George Napier's unwavering faith once again placed him in grave danger. In 1603, he had been ordained as a Catholic priest in northern France. Then, on 19 July 1610, following a tip-off, government spymasters conducted a dawn raid on his home in Kirtlington, near Woodstock. There, they discovered clear evidence of his priesthood—including a pyx containing two consecrated hosts and a small reliquary—items that were more than enough to seal his fate.

Napier was arrested and imprisoned at Oxford Castle, where he was tried and found guilty of being a Catholic priest—a capital offence at the time. He was initially sentenced to death, but was granted a temporary reprieve, likely due to his age. At sixty, he was considered relatively old by Jacobean standards.

However, two incidents soon undermined any hope of mercy. First, a convicted highwayman named Falkner claimed at his own execution that Napier had reconciled him to the Catholic Church while they were both imprisoned in Oxford Castle—a public admission that reignited suspicion. Secondly, Napier refused to swear an oath of allegiance to the king. To understand the weight of that refusal, one must remember the national climate: the country was still reeling from the Gunpowder Plot, which had been attempted just five years earlier by Catholic conspirators' intent on destroying the monarchy. The fact that part of that infamous plot had been hatched in Oxford—at the Catherine Wheel Inn on St Giles—likely did little to help Napier's case.

Napier was informed that his execution would take place at Oxford Castle on 9 November 1610. The sentence was to be hanged, drawn, and quartered—a brutal punishment reserved for those convicted of high treason. It's a phrase many of us have encountered countless times in history books on Tudor England, often without fully grasping the horrific reality behind it. I must admit, I was once guilty of this ignorance myself. Perhaps, in memory of George Napier, we owe it to him to understand the full, harrowing nature of the ordeal he endured that November day.

On the morning of his execution, Napier would have celebrated the Eucharist one final time. His appointment with the gallows was set for 1 p.m. Around midday, boisterous and abusive crowds would gather at the execution site, buzzing with anticipation for the grim spectacle to come. It's hard to imagine now, but people would travel in from the countryside for weekend trips just to witness these executions—where voyeurs could indulge their "vicarious sadistic pleasures," to quote the Oxford historian Eva Wagner.

The next stage of this horrific ordeal saw Napier tied to the scaffold, where the executioner plunged a blade into his abdomen and "drew" out his intestines. This was swiftly followed by castration—a brutal act that symbolically stripped him of his masculinity and ensured his bloodline would be forever vanquished.

Napier would then have been forced to watch as his intestines and genitals were burned before his eyes. Following this, his limbs would be tied to four horses, which were then urged to pull in different directions, tearing his body apart in a grisly display of quartering, we can only hope he was already dead before that final act.

The indignities inflicted on Napier did not end with his execution. His severed remains were boiled in a cauldron of herbs and spices to preserve them, so they could be scattered across the city gates as a stark warning to any would-be traitors. Meanwhile, his head was mounted atop the steeple of Christchurch, looming over the very city where he had been born and raised.

Centuries later, in 1929, Napier received long-overdue recognition as one of England's great Catholic martyrs when he was beatified by Pope Pius XI. The Oxford historian John Whitehead, himself a proud Catholic convert, shared with me that in 2010 a plaque honouring Napier as a martyr was unveiled at Oxford Castle. The ceremony, attended by the Archbishop of Birmingham and witnessed by a large crowd, included a blessing of the very site where Napier had been executed. [127] A just reward for Napier's unwavering faith in the face of such terror…but I can't help but wonder: does Napier truly rest in peace? Many accounts suggest otherwise.

Legend has it that Napier's family secretly recovered his severed body parts and buried them in a hidden spot in Sandford-upon-Thames, a district about five miles from Oxford. Unfortunately, according to the tale, they were unable to retrieve his head—likely due to the high walls protecting Christchurch. Perhaps this is why Napier is said to wander in and out of the shadows along Banbury Road, forever searching for his missing cranium.

As for the bones his family did manage to recover, speculation arose that they were buried in a chapel in Sandford-upon-Thames, which was later converted into a barn. However, an excavation in the early 1990s found no remains on the site, leading to the belief that Napier's bones were eventually reinterred somewhere in France. [128]

According to several reports I've come across, Napier is said to wander various parts of Oxford. While reading Betty Puttick's *Oxfordshire: Stories of the Supernatural*, I discovered that Napier is also believed to roam the

The Site of Napier's Execution.
{Photograph} Tom McDonnell

grounds of Magdalen College. Over the years, there have been multiple sightings of a figure draped in black, silently gliding across the college lawn toward the colonnade arches. Given that he is headless, the eerie silence comes as little surprise. Witnesses say the spectre vanishes into thin air as it nears the staircase.

One eyewitness recalled: "It's clothes did not move, and it made no sound at all." Another described the apparition as: "A black silhouette—which kept pace with me."

There's an intriguing connection between Napier and Magdalen College: a house owned by the college, which has been leased to various occupants over the years, once belonged to Napier himself. It's been claimed that on occasion, Napier has been seen peering out from a third-floor bedroom window—though reports don't specify whether he was seen with or without his head. [129]

Magdalen College has an undeniably eerie presence. During the summer of 2018, I spoke with three different American men who had attended a conference there. Each had stayed in college accommodation—and, curiously, each recounted the same strange experience. Though the men didn't know one another, their stories were nearly identical. All claimed to have turned off the lights before going to sleep, only to wake in the middle of the night with the lights inexplicably switched back on. They also described an unsettling sensation: the distinct feeling that someone was in the room, silently watching them.

I couldn't help but wonder if this presence might be the restless spirit of George Napier. Then again, considering the college was built on the site of a medieval monastic hospital for travellers with infectious diseases, it's likely that Magdalen has more than one ghostly resident.

During my research, I was surprised to uncover yet another legend surrounding Napier. According to this tale, he has been seen driving a ghostly coach drawn by four horses, making his way from Temple Farm toward Oxford—a route that intriguingly suggests he is journeying away from his supposed final resting place in Sandford-upon-Thames. Tradition holds a chilling warning: anyone unfortunate enough to witness this spectral carriage is said to die within a year of the sighting.[130]

So, it seems that George Napier's ghost is not confined to the Banbury Road but can be found in various corners of Oxford. And as my research continued, I discovered he is not the only ghost named George said to haunt the Banbury Road, he awaits us in the next chapter.

40.
BRUTAL GEORGE

I recently discovered an account from the mid 1970's which bore frightening similarities to a strange event I had witnessed in 2002, an incident which I had almost forgotten about until I read the story of a couple, Simon Kent and Jane Smith.

According to the Oxford ghost story collector, John Richardson, the couple were walking home from a party in the city centre late at night, true to the spirit of many classic ghost stories—the couple chose to take a short cut along a path through the graveyard, Jane decided to sit down and rest on a stone, whilst she rested, Simon noticed that Jane had suddenly become uncharacteristically quiet, eerily so, he put his arm around her and gave her a playful nudge, the reaction she gave was not exactly what Simon expected, Jane jumped up and screamed, she demanded not to be touched, she then ran at a pace along St Giles towards Broad street, Simon naturally followed her, Jane looked over her shoulder as she ran and strangely began to accuse Simon of trying to kill her, for some unknown reason, she also kept referring to him as George.

Simon apparently ran as fast as he could but could not keep up with Jane who ran like a woman possessed, literally, the end of the chase was exceptionally dramatic, when Jane reached Magdalen bridge on the High Street, she clambered onto the bridge and leapt into the river below, fortunately, Simon, aided by some people passing by, managed to rescue her, as soon as Jane was back on the safety of land, she was understandably very shaken, the report states that she continued to repeatedly utter the name George.

The following day, still baffled by the chaotic events of

the night before, Simon Kent decided to walk through St Giles' graveyard in an attempt to make sense of what had happened. He retraced his steps and located the exact stone where Jane had rested. Upon closer inspection, he realised it was actually a tombstone—carved with the name of a man called George.[131]

As I read about Tim and Jane's ordeal, it triggered a memory of something I had witnessed in the same location back in the winter of 2002. I was out on a late Sunday afternoon walk with an old friend, Laura. We had spent a few hours at the Rose and Crown pub on North Parade, and as it was getting late, we set off toward the bus station so she could catch a coach home to Witney. It's a good twenty-minute walk from the pub, so I accompanied her.

We were in good spirits, chatting and laughing, but as we passed St Giles' Church, something very strange happened. Laura suddenly froze in fear and insisted that I was taking her the wrong way. At first, I thought she was joking and laughed it off—after all, Laura had worked for a local tourism company for years and knew Oxford like the back of her hand. But I stopped laughing when, in a genuine state of panic, she flagged down a couple of strangers and asked them if we were heading in the right direction.

Once they reassured her that we were indeed on the correct route, Laura seemed to snap out of her frightened state instantly and returned to her usual cheerful self. The transformation was so sudden and complete, it was as though she had woken from a dream—or emerged from a trance. At the time, I dismissed the incident as the result of one too many gin and tonics. But reading Jane Smith's account, which took place in precisely the same spot, brought the memory flooding back. It vividly reminded me just how dramatic the change in Laura's demeanour had been that night.

Fortunately, my account is far less intense than Simon and Jane's story. Laura probably forgot the whole thing by the next morning. Still, it would have been a night etched into our memories forever had she decided to swan dive off Magdalen Bridge.

I couldn't help but find it noteworthy that Jane Smith hurled herself off the bridge while screaming the name 'George'—especially since George Napier, the Catholic martyr, is said to haunt nearby Magdalen College. Still, it seems rather unlikely that saintly George has taken a break from eternal contemplation to go chasing terrified women through Oxford like some kind of spectral Casanova with boundary issues.

I set out to investigate the identity of the man named George, buried in St Giles' Churchyard—the figure who appears to inspire such fear, and whose victims seem to possess unsuspecting women.

I assumed this investigation would be challenging. The author John Richardson, who was once acquainted with friends of mine, appears to have vanished without a trace. Most of the graves in St Giles' Churchyard are very old, with thousands of burials having taken place there. However, the last new plot was dug in 1848; any subsequent interments have been limited to existing family plots. This cessation of burials was in accordance with nationwide legislation. Beginning in the early 1840s, growing public concern over the overcrowding of churchyards prompted calls for reform. These concerns culminated in legislative changes during the 1850s, which led to the development of municipal cemeteries and, eventually, crematoria across England.

More than a dozen individuals named George are buried in St Giles, but the first hurdle was surprisingly easy to overcome. Thanks to the flat design of the tombstones and their close proximity to Banbury Road, the possibilities quickly narrowed to just three: George Wood, George Parrott Sr and George Parrott Jr. The latter two—a father and son—are buried in the same plot, alongside the family matriarch, Mary, and a daughter, Catherine Sarah.

> George Parrott buried 1854, aged 55
> Mary Parrott buried 1858, aged 56
> George Thomas Parrot buried 1866, aged 35
> Catherine Sarah Parrott buried 1902, aged 68

Graves of men who may hold secrets.
{Photograph} Tom McDonnell

Curious to discover whether George Parrott or his son had any criminal history, I began my investigation. To my surprise, I found that in pre-Victorian times, convicted murderers were indeed allowed to be buried in churchyards. However, their burial plots were typically allocated on the north side of the church—the side then considered the least spiritual. Notably, the tombstone of George Parrott and his family is located on the respectable south side, suggesting no such stigma was attached to them.

While trawling through old documents at the Oxfordshire History Centre, I discovered that George Parrot the Elder had been a farmer and dairyman. He lived directly opposite St Giles' Church, on the east side, at 28 Keble Road—in a house that was later demolished to make way for the old Mathematical Institute.

George the Elder must have been a man of considerable means, he owned 73 acres of land and employed eight labourers. He died in 1854, and his wife Mary passed away just four years later. Between 19 November 1859 and 19 January 1860, the farm was sold off in a piecemeal fashion to the farming partnership of Stanley Lowe and William Heydon. I would assume the land was divided and sold in stages due to extended negotiations with Mrs. Hudson, the farm's trustee.

Their son, George Thomas Parrott, must have fared well from the sale of the farm, his official status was listed as 'gentleman.' He died in 1866 at the young age of thirty-five, not long after the passing of his parents. Before his untimely death, George married and had a son, whom he named George Richard Parrott—unsurprisingly continuing the family tradition.

George Richard Parrott also lived opposite St Giles' Church, though on the west side, in Wellington Square. He was described as a gentleman of private means, with no listed occupation. In his later years, he took up residence at the exclusive Clarendon Hotel on Cornmarket Street, which was demolished in 1954 [132] He lived to the ripe old age of 74, though sadly, his final days were spent in the Warneford psychiatric hospital, where he died on 15 August 1933. His funeral was held at St Giles' Church two days later. Curiously, however, the location of his burial remains a mystery. His son served as his executor—and, unsurprisingly, was also named George.

My research has revealed an intriguing portrait of a rural Oxford family who gradually rose through the social ranks—from their humble beginnings as hardworking farmers to attaining the status of gentlemen. It seems that most of the Parrott men chose to remain within the parish of St Giles, lived relatively short lives, and shared a distinct lack of imagination when it came to naming their sons.

There does not appear to be any scandals attached to the Parrott family, in fact, quite the opposite. In 1849, George Parrott the Elder served as a witness in a case where three felons were accused of pilfering a hamper from a carrier's cart as it travelled from St Giles to North Oxford. For the record, the cart contained forty pounds of butter, one hundred oranges, and eleven pounds of mutton, it was certainly a crime from a bygone era.

The only other possible suspect named George who could have inspired such fear in the young women of Oxford was George Wood, a property magnate from Summertown who died in 1830 at the age of just forty-three.

Shortly after his death, an auction took place at the Mitre Inn, offering nine freehold dwelling houses in the parishes of St Ebbes and St Clement's for sale. Yet, once again, there's nothing in the records to suggest he was a man of foul temperament or questionable character.

So, without wishing to cast aspersions on the Parrott family who can't defend themselves or sully the reputation of George Wood, it is with great dissatisfaction that I had to mark this case as unsolved, and although the identity of this terrifying man remains a mystery, it's seems as though the spirits of his victims still occasionally possess the living who are brave enough to pass through St Giles graveyard at night.

Our time spent prodding the strange past of St Giles graveyard is far from over, there is said to be yet another ghost wandering around the gravestones, we shall come to her in the final chapter.

Dead but Awake

41.
THE BOSWELL INCIDENT

The Store is a relatively new hotel located on Broad Street, occupying the historic site of a shop, Boswells & Co, once the second-oldest department store in England. A cherished Oxford institution, Boswells was established in 1738 and served generations of locals and visitors for over two centuries.

However, the rise of online shopping and the convenience of home delivery for pharmaceuticals all played a role in Boswells' closure in 2019.

Many staff members were understandably saddened by the closure—and one can only imagine the sense of enforced loneliness it brought to George, the shop's resident ghost.

I know many people who have worked at Boswells, and over the decades staff have reported all sorts of strange occurrences in the shop. My friend Bahram once told me that, according to local lore, a pharmacist named George had worked there — until the day he tragically fell, or perhaps jumped, down a lift shaft.[133]

Another former employee, Salli, recalled that many staff had noticed the lift in the toy department behaving strangely — opening and closing on its own. Some couldn't help but wonder if George was involved.[134]

There was also the case of a man who worked in the stockroom and flat-out refused to enter a particular section, claiming it had an oppressive atmosphere. He said he constantly felt as though someone was watching him.[135]

However, something doesn't quite add up with the legend of George, having meticulously looked through the British newspaper archives, I have found no reports whatsoever of any accidental deaths in the old shop.

Which leads me to another candidate for the ghost of Boswells.

Directly outside the site of the old shop, three prominent churchmen, Thomas Cranmer, Nicholas Ridley, and Hugh Latimer, were burned alive for their Protestant faith. Their execution took place during the reign of Mary I, known to history as "Bloody Mary." Her father, Henry VIII, had famously broken from the Church of Rome to divorce her mother, Katherine of Aragon. But when Mary came to power, she was determined to restore Catholicism in England—and would go to bloody lengths to do so.

After overseeing the deaths of dozens of Protestant martyrs in London, Queen Mary turned her attention to Oxford, where three influential Protestant bishops were imprisoned and tried for heresy. Latimer and Ridley were found guilty and, on the morning of 16 October 1555, were chained to the stake and burned on Broad Street.

Cranmer was forced to stand and watch helplessly as his friends burnt to death.

According to some sources, Latimer, old and resolute, raised his voice above the crackling of the kindling and cried out:

"Be of good comfort, Master Ridley, and play the man; we shall this day light such a candle, by God's grace, in England as I trust shall never be put out."

It wasn't long before the smoke fumes put Latimer's lights out.

A popular tale, often recounted by tour guides—claims that Latimer's friends sewed an excessive amount of gunpowder into his clothing to hasten his death. According to legend, the explosion was so forceful that his head flew into Balliol College.

It took nearly two hours for the flames to reach Ridley's waist—an unimaginable agony. When the fire finally caught hold, it burned with such ferocity that the wooden doors of Balliol College across the street were scorched by the heat. Those very doors were later removed and preserved; they now hang quietly in Balliol's central quad as a silent witness to the past.

The door of Cranmer's prison cell also still survives and is now on display at St Michael at the Northgate — the church that stood beside the long-vanished prison which once held him.[136]

Cranmer's day of reckoning came the following year, in March 1556. Once a powerful Archbishop under Henry VIII, Thomas Cranmer spent his final days imprisoned in the Bocardo Prison above Oxford's North Gate. From his cell, he had a constant view of the very spot where he would meet his fate.

On the day of his trial at the University Church, Cranmer recanted and signed a confession, hoping for clemency. But there would be none—it was a show trial, its outcome predetermined. He was led from the church to the stake, to the very spot where his friends had perished. In a final act of defiance, Cranmer renounced his recantation and, as the flames rose, he thrust his right hand into the fire—the hand that had signed the recantation

"This hand," he cried, "hath offended." And thus, Thomas Cranmer died—his final act speaking louder than the words he had just signed.[137]

A cross that supposedly marks the site of the execution stands outside the Store Hotel. But what does all this have to do with the ghost said to haunt the old department store? Well, I discovered on Tony Morris's excellent Oxford history website that Simon Ballard, Keeper of the Saxon Tower at St Michael at the North Gate, believes the cross may not mark the exact spot of the execution.

According to Simon;

"The cross in Broad Street acts as a marker for the woeful burning of Cranmer and his Bishops; but the actual site was in a line of ditch where what was once Boswells department store stands. It would have been just outside the North Gate entrance, a deliberately ignominious spot.

A woodcut also shows that it wasn't from the Bocardo Prison that Cranmer was forced to witness the burning of Bishops Latimer and Ridley, but in fact the adjacent Devil's Tower. A blow-up of this woodcut can be seen in the Saxon Tower on Cornmarket Street."[138]

The spherical tower from which, according to the woodcut, Cranmer watched his friends burn still exists today, tucked away behind the Store Hotel and incorporated into Jesus College. Over the years, it has been known by many names — the Martyr's Bastion, Cranmer's Bastion, and, most intriguingly, the Devil's Tower.

I know Simon Ballard; we share a passion for horror films, and we both agreed that "the Devil's Tower" is an unusual name for this kind of structure. After all, according to legend, it's notoriously difficult for a devil or demon to hide in a spherical building.[139]

George in all likelihood was merely a term of endearment for the spectre of the old shop, and let's face it, according to my research it seems to be a very popular name for ghosts in Oxford, it could well be the case that the paranormal activity is down to those clergy men who suffered such a horrible fate on the site of Boswells and Co.

42.
THE BOY WITH THE LANTERN

In Chapter 39, I referenced the legend of George Napier's ghost, said to haunt the grounds of Magdalen College. However, during a conversation in December 2023 with Nick Swarbrick—an Oxford Brookes University lecturer and Magdalen alumnus—I learned that Napier is not the only spirit associated with the college.

Nick, who studied at Magdalen during the 1980s, recalled that at the time, the most famous ghost was not Napier, but a mysterious boy with a lantern. This figure was reportedly only ever seen from a distance, drifting through the college grounds. Some believed the light came from an old-fashioned lantern, while others claimed it wasn't a lantern at all, but rather a glowing will-o'-the-wisp—an otherworldly spirit said to float across from Angel Meadow, a large floodplain situated beneath Magdalen Bridge.

Legends of the will-o'-the-wisp appear in many cultures, each with its own interpretation. In European folklore, such lights are often thought to be the souls of stillborn or unbaptised children, flickering between the boundaries of heaven and hell.

I couldn't help but wonder if there might be any likely candidates for Magdalen's lantern-carrying ghost, well, the college is rumored to be haunted by the ghost of Oscar Wilde, who likely lit up Magdalen with his brilliance while studying classics there in the 1870's.

Wilde managed to achieve a double first despite being fined on numerous occasions for being absent, which is quite ironic given that he's now reportedly confined to never leave the college. Wilde certainly liked to turn heads at Oxford, he would often stroll along the high street, walking his pet on a lead, not a pet dog but a pet lobster, perhaps the boy with the lantern is the ghost of Wilde, staggering back from a tavern, having engaged in a spirited debate with his peers, and perhaps having had one drink too many, relying on his lantern to light his way back to his room in the dark, it's a romantic idea, but it's likely that we will never discover the true identity of the mysterious boy.

As for Nick Swarbrick, no matter how hard he strained his eyes, he never managed to catch a glimpse of the mysterious boy with the lantern[140]

43.
THE LAMENTABLE TALE OF JOHN CROCKER

I've organised a great number of jazz and folk concerts in churches across Oxford. With congregations dwindling, many of these places of worship now double up as concert venues to help fund essential repairs. One such venue is the magnificent St John the Evangelist Church on Iffley Road, which happens to overlook the university running track where Sir Roger Bannister famously broke the four-minute mile.

In the summer of 2015, I attended a garden party at the church, where I found myself in an absorbing conversation with the novelist Richard Doyle. He shared with me details of an unusual social event held annually at Lincoln College, where he had studied back in the 1960s, according to Richard...

"Lincoln College has a long-standing rivalry with its neighbour Brasenose, the two colleges share a tradition which is revived annually on Ascension Day, legend has it that many centuries ago, as a mob of locals chased students through the streets of Oxford, the porter of Lincoln allowed the Lincoln students to enter and escape the gang, however, the porter refused entry to a Brasenose man, leaving him at the mercy of the mob, the poor chap was beaten to a pulp.

Every year since the student's death, on Ascension Day, Lincoln invite members of Brasenose College over for a beer as a penance, the Brasenose contingent enter through the one door which connects the two colleges, it is the only occasion that the door is ever used"[141]

This story intrigued me, as I'd heard of a similar fate that befell John Crocker, an Exeter College student in the

17th century. According to tradition, Crocker was beaten to death by a mob of townspeople on Turl Street after he unsuccessfully tried to seek refuge in Lincoln College. Exeter, like Lincoln, borders Turl Street—though the two colleges are separated by a narrow lane.

In 1916, Thomas Wood, an Exeter college student, claimed to have seen the ghost of John Crocker, Wood was at the time a member of a now defunct student society, The Unbelievers Club, an ironic name, given what reportedly happened on 31 October.

The effigy of John Crocker.
{Photograph} Iain Stevenson

This account is best delivered straight from the pen of the witness, Dr Thomas Wood;

ON STAIRCASE SIX

The Unbelievers' Club used to meet at half-past ten every Tuesday in the Michaelmas Term and the Hilary Term for a binge. It was a mild sort of binge – a bingeling, or a binganniny – of coffee and baccy and talk, and everyone brought his own sugar. This was 1916. Nearly all the men in College were members of the Unbelievers' Club. There was no subscription. There were no rules; and not one single noble cause was a rallying-point, even Unbelief. We met at one another's rooms in turn; pulled up round the fire, and smoked all blue.

It was a gusty rainy night. I got back to College late. P. T. Williams was waiting in the lodge, balancing himself first on one foot and then the other as he always did when he was cold. He looked at his watch.

'Brace up, Tom, and get your sugar p.d.q. It's twenty-five past.'

I doubled across the gravel – the front quad at Exeter was not grassed then – and went up No. 6 staircase two steps at a time, five flights. My rooms were at the top. Not a soul about. All the men must have gone over to Irving's room. But Sharp was working. He had sported his oak. A good old slogger, Sharp. Safe for a Second. No Unbelievers' Club for him tonight. I slung off my overcoat and gown, grabbed the sugar-basin and tucked it under my arm in the exasperation of hurry – the door had blown to.

Quick, now! One hand for the knob, the other for the switch – turn and press up together: and the light was out, the door was open, and I was half over the threshold, to stop, frozen. A man was standing right up against me with the narrow band of light under Sharp's door shining through his body, and he had no head.

Words won't come fast enough. Buff coat: yellow slashings: black gown: one hand up as though he were going to knock; man-broad, man- high, rock-still, clean-cut, vivid: the bright pinpoint of Sharp's keyhole where his heart should be and where his face should be, nothing. He stood while I could have counted one, two, three, four; and my hair bristled. My scalp was sore next day. Then he went – puff – out like a candle. And I took one jump over that threshold and was down the stairs in the next best thing to a headlong fall.

P. T. Williams was waiting at the bottom, still balancing himself on one foot and then the other. He stopped to stare at me.

'Anything the matter?'

'That's what I want to know. Look here, P. T., what b.f. tricks have you been up to this time?'

P. T. was reading for the Honour School of Theology. As an offset he had acquired to perfection the little gesture of mock-modesty that looks so well upon the stage, and the roguish eye that goes with it.

'Tut, tut! Tuts in two spots. You shock me, my Thomas. I have previously had occasion to reprove this indulgence in strong language – sad, too, in one so young.'

'Blast your neck, P. T.! What have you been doing in my room?'

'I've not been near your room. "My hands are clean – my brow serene – I've nothing to conceal, old bean" – neat, that.' P. T. turned a graceful pirouette.

'But why this vile and slanderous insinuagger? Anything wrong with your room?'

'Yes. Someone's been playing hanky-panky with it – just outside it, anyway.'

'Why accuse me?'

'You're the only practical joker in College. I mean to say – '

'I have seized opportunities, I admit – 'P. T. put on his Private Secretary voice – 'to display my well-known histrionic gifts as impersonator and –

"Dry up, P. T. This is serious. I think I've seen a ghost.'

P. T. stopped dead. 'Then why the hell didn't you say so before? Where?'

'Outside my room, I tell you.'

'Just now?'

'Yes.'

'But you weren't up there more than a jiff – I'd only time to walk across the quad.'

'I can't help that. I saw something dam' rum.' 'Is it there now?'

No. Yes. I'm not sure.'

'Did it look like a ghost?'

'Yes'

'Come on! We'll have the bags off it.'

We searched. We broke in on Sharp and made him join us. We searched again: turned out the coal bin and the scout's cupboard, struck 27 matches. We switched the lights on and off: we experimented with the doors: we brought a looking-glass: we smelt in long and inquiring sniffs. No. There was nothing on the landing that could have turned itself into a ghost, nothing that bore the mark of one. Even the smell was the normal blend of autumn fog, Oxford damp, and that refined and academic mildew which hangs about a college staircase. Sharp was as puzzled as I was. Had he seen anything? Why, no-o. He'd just been sitting around. He'd heard me come along and he'd heard me go away. He guessed he didn't take much stock in ghosts. They didn't raise ghosts back home in Indiana. It was easy to believe this; and just as easy to believe that Sharp, gentle old solemn-eyed Sharp, was the last person who would think of spoofing one.

We fetched the Unbelievers' Club in a body from Bill Irving's room on No. 7, and they came shouting. A ghost-hunt was something new. But their united intelligence produced no explanation that was satisfactory, and they fell back on humour of the accepted sort: drank my health in coffee. Any chap, they said, who could fudge up a yarn like that all in a minute and a quarter and without the help of alcohol – well, he was a credit to the Unbelievers' Club.

At ten next morning – Wednesday – I had a logic lecture. It was the Bursar who took me in logic. He was A. B. Howl, a large and kindly man, rather shy, who had rowed 4 in the Exeter boat that won the Grand in 1882, and still kept the frame and bearing of an oarsman. No-one, ever, had bigger wrists. I liked him.

Everybody did. It was his custom when logic was done with to talk, gently, on general topics – the news of the day, my chances in the schools, autumn colouring. On this particular morning, he told me about the work that had been started under No. 6 staircase – mine. The present coal-cellar was not big enough, and they were clearing the junk and rubble of centuries out of the basement to get more room. Last night they had made a discovery. It was a statue of a man in seventeenth-century dress, rather knocked about, but of distinct archaeological interest. Would I care to see it?

had cleared a space in the basement and ranged along the wall in orderly lines lumps of weathered stone and big carved blocks that might have been part of a cornice. Standing on one of them was the statue. It was just visible in the light that came through the area grating. I had expected something bigger. This was tiny. It showed a man kneeling in the attitude of prayer. He was wearing his gown and a tunic that had slashed sleeves edged with lace round the wrists. Faint traces of colour were left: brown. He had no head. My hair bristled for the second time. I had seen the original of this battered bit of marble. He came last night to knock at my door.

The statue appears to be identical with a monument put up to the memory of John Crocker, a gentleman-commoner of Exeter College and the only son of John Crocker of Devon, knight. He died on April 29th, 1629. The authority is a passage which states that in Exeter College chapel 'against the south wall, is the proportion of a young man kneeling in a gown, depicted to the life, with this inscription under him': . . . Sixteen lines of somewhat involved Latin follow, setting out his virtues.

This chapel was the second the College has had. The first was built in 1321-6 and lasted three hundred years. The next was built in 1623-4 and lasted two hundred years. It would probably be standing yet if a craze for modern Gothic had not bitten laymen and architects alike in the '50's. Anyone can be wise after the event; but on principle, ladies and gentlemen, distrust fanatics; most of all those fanatics who preach what they call a Faith. By the time they have got to this stage they have lost all feeling for proportion and their common sense as well.

In ten year – 1854-1864 – men of that type ruined the Jacobean chapel of Jesus College, pulled down the Jacobean chapel at Balliol College and pulled down the Jacobean Chapel at Exeter College. At Exeter the fabric was said to be unsafe. This must have been good news to anyone who wished to try this nice new modern Gothic; and so, George Hakewill's chapel was condemned. It was he who was Rector in 1623; and he gave twelve hundred pounds towards the cost of this chapel although he had 'two sons of his own to be provided for'. They might have known in 1854 that this sort of man would have got his money's worth. Too late, they found that he had done so. There is a College tradition that gun- powder had to be used before this unsafe fabric was finally razed. The masonry of the old chapel went to make the foundations of the new; and some mouldings, a few blocks of stone, and the statue of John Crocker were probably carried into the cellar of No. 6 staircase and forgotten.

The statue was found during the afternoon of October 31st, 1916. I saw John Crocker at half-past ten that night. I heard about him for the first time at about eleven o'clock next morning. I do not know why he came to me, or why he came to that particular room, or why he came without his head. It is most unlikely that there is any family connexion; his manner of death cannot be traced, and wherever his rooms may have been in college they were not on No. 6 staircase. It forms part of an extension built in 1708 on the site of an older building. I have no explanation to offer. I am not prepared to invent one.

The experts in such matters tell me that true ghost stories are like that: pointless. I have no views. I have simply given the facts."
Thomas Wood [142]

So, there we have Thomas Woods fascinating account of a sighting which took place on Halloween 1916. A most appropriate day to meet a ghost.

We know that Crocker was born in Devon in 1629, but the official cause of his death remains as elusive today as it was in Wood's time. Perhaps the legend of his murder at the hands of a local mob is just that… a legend.

As for Thomas Wood, he was rejected from military service in the First World War due to poor eyesight. In the early 1920s, he returned to Exeter College as a music lecturer and later achieved great success as a composer and author.

A devoted collector of folk songs and a self-proclaimed australophile, Wood was especially captivated by 'Waltzing Matilda.' His arrangement of the song played a key role in popularising it as Australia's unofficial anthem[143]

His 1940 book *Cobbers Campaigning*, a tribute to Australia's war efforts during the Second World War, proved wildly popular and was reprinted eleven times during his lifetime., Despite his public success, Wood remained deeply fascinated by the supernatural. In his later years, after retiring to Parsonage Hall in the village of Bures, Suffolk, he wrote extensively about ghostly encounters.[144]

I must say, I disagree with Woods' criticism of Exeter's chapel. From his description, you'd imagine a garish eyesore. While the Victorians were certainly capable of architectural monstrosities, Exeter's Chapel is not one of them, quite the opposite, in fact, and well worth a visit. Designed by George Gilbert Scott and inspired by the Sainte-Chapelle in Paris, the chapel features a glorious tapestry by William Morris and Edward Burne-Jones adorning the wall beside the altar

Before the 2020 pandemic, the headless statue of John Crocker was on display in the chapel. For reasons unclear, it now languishes on a farm owned by the college somewhere in North Oxford, there are whispers that a former chaplain felt uncomfortable about the statue being in the chapel.[145]

The statue is a small yet strangely powerful effigy of a young scholar whose dreams were tragically cut short, a symbol of a restless soul, one who, even in death, seems to have found no peace.

44.
THE MAN WITH THE TWINKLE IN HIS EYE

Most ghosts, according to the reports I've come across, appear to mechanically reenact moments from their lifetimes, seemingly unaware of the living around them. That's why I'm always intrigued by the rarer accounts of spirits that do interact with the living. In April 2024, I spoke with a woman whose family lived in Denchworth—a small village a few miles north of Wantage. They resided in a house dating back to the 17th century, which once served as a village shop.

She told me that on one occasion, while reading in bed with the bedside lamp on, she suddenly became aware of a small, elderly man standing beside her bed. Strangely, he appeared just as surprised to see her as she was to see him.

She turned away, hoping it was a trick of the light—but when she looked back, the man was still there. She looked away again, and when she finally dared to face him once more, he had vanished without a trace.

The following day, she told her mother about the visitation, her mother asked, "Was it a small old man with a cheerful twinkle in his eyes?"

When the daughter confirmed this to be an accurate description, her mother told her that she had recently seen the same mysterious man in her hand mirror as she applied her make up, fortunately, the family didn't feel particularly threatened by the ghostly old man as he seemed to be so cheerful.

Purely speculation, but I did wonder if it might have been the ghost of Arthur Dearlove who passed away at the age of 85, 27 August 1957, in his day Dearlove was a pillar of the Denchworth community, he was elected church warden, acted as secretary of the parochial church council, was employed as a school manager and for many years managed the post office, a position which was later occupied by his son.

Perhaps Arthur's returned to sort through the letters of yesteryear, wandering around the house with the cheerful demeanour which one may naturally attach to the village postmaster of popular imagination.

I was fascinated to discover that my friend, the historian Marilyn Yurdan, had noted in her book on the paranormal that...

"Near Letcombe Brook, on the outskirts of the town, lives the gentlest ghost, as *The Didcot Advertiser* {January 2 -1959} calls the little old man who may be encountered there".[146]

Letcombe Brook is only two miles from Denchworth, could it be that this gentle old man is perpetually wandering through his old stomping ground, keeping a watch on his old haunts with a twinkle in his eye.

45.
TREATMENT OF DEAD ENEMIES

During the winter of 2018, I struck up a conversation with a gentleman named Mark Bolden, a frequent visitor to Oxford. He happened to be in the city that day to tour its museums. When I mentioned, in passing, that I was researching for a book on ghosts, his eyes lit up. He went on to recount a strange experience he'd had at the Pitt Rivers Museum on Parks Road, something he had witnessed nearly twenty-five years earlier.

The Pitt Rivers Museum is home to the remarkable collection of its founder, the Victorian general Augustus Pitt-Rivers. Connected to the Natural History Museum and nestled beside the expansive University Parks, it's one of Oxford's must-see destinations.

Many of the museum's artefacts were collected during Captain James Cook's exploratory voyages through the South Pacific. Cook's pursuit of exploration ultimately led to his downfall, when he was killed during a violent altercation with Hawaiian islanders in 1779.

At first, the islanders believed Cook and his crew to be gods, as their arrival coincided with the local annual fertility festival. However, when a storm forced Cook's ship to return shortly after departing, the illusion was shattered, revealing him to be no more than a mere mortal, this revelation also left him vulnerable to the sharp end of a dagger and the blunt force of many clubs.[147]

Today, we are acutely aware that many display cabinets in British museums are filled with artefacts forcefully acquired by English explorers. The origins of these vitrines of curiosity remain firmly rooted in the histories of countless, voiceless victims of British colonial ambition. In that light, the Pitt Rivers Museum holds a certain irony: it owes its existence to the legacy of a colonising Westerner who, in the end, was himself claimed by the very world he sought to dominate.

Back to Mark's story: he recalled admiring a collection of Peruvian artefacts when he was suddenly struck by the eerie sensation of being watched. Glancing over his shoulder, he saw a woman staring at him with an intense, unwavering glare, Mark described her as a woman with an olive complexion, strikingly dressed in what seemed to be a tribal outfit, adorned with a beaded necklace. Without saying a word, she gave him a maniacal grin before wandering off, by the time Mark fully registered what had just happened, the grinning woman had already vanished from sight, baffled by the woman's sudden disappearance, Mark searched the museum from end to end. His efforts, however, were in vain, there was no trace of her anywhere. Feeling somewhat perplexed, he approached several of the museum's staff to inquire whether a special interactive event had been planned for that afternoon, perhaps with costumed actors roaming the exhibits, but it transpired that no such program was scheduled for that day. Still, Mark was utterly convinced he had seen the mysterious woman. He also remembered it being a bitterly cold day and noted that she had been dressed in a way that was entirely unsuitable for the weather.[148]

I found the story even more intriguing when Mark described the collection he had been viewing at the time of the encounter—a cabinet labelled *'Treatment of Dead Enemies.'* The display featured a wide array of human remains from around the world, including shrunken heads known as tsantsa, which originated in the Upper Amazon region of South America and Ecuador and were crafted by the ancient Shuar and Achuar tribes. The shrunken heads on display were genuine artifacts of this ritual tradition.

I was surprised to discover just how much skill is

required to produce a shrunken head. The process begins by carefully peeling the skin and hair from the skull, which is then discarded. The detached skin is then boiled, after which hot sand is poured into the cavity to help it retain its shape. The facial features are then meticulously reshaped, the eyes and mouth sewn shut with cotton string, the face darkened with dye, and the finished head strung onto a cord.

The Achuar and Shuar people believed that a man possessed more than one soul. The purpose of the tsantsas was to capture the spiritual power of an enemy's soul. This captured power was then harnessed by the victor to strengthen themselves; they also believed that this spiritual power could be harnessed to ensure bountiful harvests.

For many years, the tsantsas were among the most controversial objects on display in any of the city's museums. For decades, the Shuar and Achuar tribes had called for their return, believing the heads rightfully belonged to them. What the tribes regarded as objects of deep spiritual reverence had been reduced to mere curiosities, sideshow attractions for selfie stick waving tourists to gawk at.

Interestingly, in 1998, Cambridge University returned its collection of tsantsas, which had been on display at the Fitzwilliam Museum for decades, Oxford, on the other hand, was far less receptive to similarly impassioned appeals, showing a marked reluctance to follow Cambridge's example.

Perhaps the spectre of the grinning lady was the restless spirit of a Peruvian shaman, desperate to see her tribe's sacred artefacts returned home. If so, she would likely have been heartened by the outcome of a three-year ethical review launched by the Pitt Rivers Museum in 2018.

This ethical rethink was in part, due to the reactions of visitors to the museum, according to the museum's director

Laura Van Broekhoven "Our audience research has shown that visitors often saw the human remains as a testament to other cultures being 'savage', 'primitive' or 'gruesome'.

"Rather than enabling our visitors to reach a deeper understanding of each other's ways of being, the displays reinforced racist and stereotypical thinking that goes against the museum's values today. The removal of the human remains also brings us in line with sector guidelines and code of ethics"[149]

The coronavirus lockdowns of 2020 gave many museums an opportunity to restructure their exhibits, it also gave the Pitt-Rivers a chance to accelerate their work on the decolonisation of the museum, at the time of writing this chapter {2021} the museum is in the process of not only removing all 2,800 human remains from its display cabinets, but also actively reaching out to descendant communities for guidance on the most appropriate way to care for the objects, including repatriation if so requested.

We may never know why Mark Bolden was seemingly singled out by the mysterious woman, but he continues to return to the museum every year, checking in with the staff to ask whether anyone else has reported sightings of the grinning lady, the answer has always been no, at least so far.

Coincidentally, just a few days before hearing Mark recount his story, I had visited the Victor Wynd Museum in Bethnal Green, London, a place not for the faint of heart. Its cosy, dimly lit rooms are crammed with bizarre and mind-boggling curiosities, among them an exceptionally rare specimen: the shrunken head of a Caucasian man, said to be the grim result of a stranger's wrong turn while navigating a river in Peru. It was a week in which the imagery of shrunken heads had etched an indelible mark on my mind, not exactly the most pleasant of images to dwell on.

46
HANKERING FOR THE GLORY DAYS

Although it was a relatively poor institution at its founding in 1555, St John's College is now one the wealthiest colleges in Oxford. According to legend, one could travel all the way from Oxford to Cambridge without ever stepping off land owned by St John's. Like many Oxford colleges, it was built on the site of an old monastery. In fact, the chapel predates the college by twenty-five years and was a functioning place of worship when the area was occupied by the Cistercian brotherhood.

The college founder, Thomas White, was a Catholic and friend to Queen Mary, as he was the head of the Merchant Taylor's school in London, he dedicated his college to the patron Saint of tailors, St John the Baptist.

Several controversial figures have studied at St John's such as Philip Larkin, the Martyr Edmund Campion and the former Prime minister Tony Blair, whose student days saw him play guitar in a band called *The Ugly Rumours*, some might suggest that the group had quite an apt name.

If one wanders around this glorious College, past the Front quadrangle and chapel, you will find yourself standing in the Canterbury Quadrangle, it is one of the most beautiful quadrangles in Oxford and is renowned as the first example of Italian renaissance architecture in Oxford,

The Canterbury Quadrangle was funded by the Archbishop of Canterbury, William Laud, the chancellor of the college and fierce supporter of King Charles, it is perhaps no coincidence that the Royalist generals would gather in the Canterbury Quadrangle to discuss their military tactics during the English Civil war.

In 1634, eight years prior to the war which soaked Oxfordshire in blood, the construction of Canterbury quadrangle was completed, within the quadrangle there is a reminder of the glory days of the king, facing each other on east and west facing walls are the statues of King Charles I and his wife, Henrietta Maria, positioned as though gazing lovingly at one another across the lawn of the Quadrangle.

Archbishop Laud was an ambitious man and a powerful figure in Oxford during the Reformation, but he made a fatal mistake by commissioning a statue of the Virgin Mary to be built in the front of the porch of the university church. The puritans at the time intensely disapproved of any symbols of devotion to Mary, this was enough to have the archbishop arrested in 1640.

Laud spent most of the Civil War imprisoned in the Tower of London where he languished four years, in what likely amounted to a show trial he was found guilty of treason and beheaded on Tower Hill in 1645, his corpse was sent to St Johns college where he was buried underneath the chapel, but it is believed that he is not at rest, for he is said to wander the halls of St John's, candle in hand, kicking his severed head in front of him, sometimes even bowling his head through the library, some people believe he's walking around looking for his head.

In the 1990's there was a student at St Johns who struggled to sleep. He got up in the night and was walking around the Canterbury quadrangle when he suddenly saw a candlelight flickering slowly across the library windows – the flame flickered slowly, and he watched it flickering across and then back again as though someone was pacing up and down the hall of the library. He wondered who could have possibly been roaming around so late at night, so he went to the library the next day and spoke with the librarian, who was in charge of the only set of keys, the librarian was adamant that he'd given them to no one.

On another night in the 1990's, four students were playing cards together when they suddenly heard someone shout "The feet", they found a shaken student who lived under the library, when they managed to calm him down he said he'd woken up to see legs and feet walking across the ceiling of his room near the library. The library floor had initially been on a lower level, so William Laud is believed to still walk on the level of the original floor.

Perhaps the poor old Archbishop is fated to eternally languish at St John's College, forever yearning for the glory days of old—before war swept through the streets of Oxford. Speaking of war, two curious incidents were reported at St John's during the Second World War, a time when many university buildings were requisitioned by the military.

In one account, the wife of a colonel fell into a trance and claimed to be "transported back to the English Civil War". She described witnessing regiments of Cavaliers lined up outside for inspection. Among them stood a small figure wearing a large velvet hat adorned with a long feather— who appeared to be overseeing the troops. She believed this man to be none other than Charles I himself.

Around the same time, The R.A.F had converted one of the college rooms into an enlistment office and several new recruits claimed that an unusual man would pass them on the staircase, a slight man dressed in 17th century clothing and once again, assumed to have been the ghost of Charles I.[150]

So, it seems that the old friends, Charles I and William Laud have been reunited in death, if only poor Laud could be reunited with his cranium.

Dead but Awake

47.
THE OLD LADY OF ST GILES

St Giles Graveyard, home to the ghost of the sobbing Lady
{Photograph} Tom McDonnell

And so, we come to the end of our journey through the darkest corners of Oxfordshire and what an array of ghosts we've encountered: murdered students, heartbroken teenagers, angry monks, and spiteful poltergeists. But before I bid you farewell, I leave you with perhaps the saddest tale of them all.

The story of yet another spirit said to haunt the St Giles area of Oxford, drifting through a paranormal cosmos between the two headless ghosts of William Laud and George Napier. It is within the churchyard of St Giles that this tragic figure is said to dwell.

I must mention that St Giles' Church is a lovely building—one of the oldest in the city, built in 1120, predating the University by several decades. Saint Giles, according to folklore, was the patron saint of prostitutes, lepers, and beggars—a clearly charitable figure. Fittingly, the church often hosts fundraising concerts for the War Child charity. Its 'Jazz at St Giles' series has featured world-class artists such as Pete Oxley, Jacqui Dankworth, and The Brickwork Lizards.

I attended one such concert on a cold winter's night in 2017. During the interval, I took a quiet stroll through the graveyard, reflecting on a legend long associated with the place. As I wandered among the tombstones, I listened intently, hoping to hear the ghostly murmur that others have apparently heard. Alas, it was not to be, all I could hear was some chap blowing his own trumpet, literally, it was a jazz concert after all.

The strange sound I sought in the darkness is said to emanate from an elderly lady, a lady who died a very long time ago.

According to tradition, it is the ghost of a kind woman who lived in the parish of St Giles, who charitably bequeathed her savings to St Giles Church, however, the terms of her will were not executed and the church received no monies from her estate, some believe that her worthy plan was discovered by scheming relatives who stole all her assets before she had a chance to have a will written, and the poor kind-hearted old woman died impoverished.

The Oxford based ghost story collector John Richardson has been collecting local supernatural accounts since the 1970s, a Mr Parker gave him an account his

Grandfather had told him in 1906, the story goes that on one evening in the Autumn of 1906, around 7pm, Mr Parker's Grandfather made his way into town from his home in the nearby neighbourhood of Jericho, he crossed over the road from little Clarendon street and strolled alongside St Giles church, which at that time was protected by a thick stone wall, surmounted by iron railings, the gentlemen saw a lady on the other side of the railings, inside the church yard, she was walking about ten metres ahead of him, it was noted that she was dressed entirely in grey, her outfit consisted of a long skirt, a cape and a wide brimmed hat and her face was obscured by a veil.

One can only imagine how shaken up Parkers grandfather was when the lady suddenly turned right and marched straight through the stone wall and the iron railings, she then headed towards what is presently the Quakers meeting house, but in 1906, was the Registrar of Births, Deaths and Marriages.

The lady didn't manage to reach the building, when she walked past a cluster of trees on the far side of the street, she simply vanished into thin air. It was around this time that several sightings of the grey lady were reported, and her apparition became the subject of popular local folk lore.[151]

Some people believe that the grey lady still haunts the graveyard of St Giles, doomed to wander amongst the tombstones, and if you were to visit the graveyard on a quiet evening, when the traffic is barely audible and the wind blows gently, listen attentively, you might just catch the sad tones of the grey lady's lonesome weeping.

And it could be said, that although the grey lady is long dead, she is dead but… seemingly awake!

Sleep well gentle reader…

Dead but Awake

EPILOGUE

Across a period of ten years, dozens of seemingly rational, level-headed people have told me about their brushes with the supernatural.

Could they all have been mistaken? Were their minds merely playing tricks on them? Was that ghastly apparition in the bathroom just a reflection in the mirror after a prolonged cocktail hour? Was the strange mist outside the old chapel just the vicar having a cheeky fag?

The people I've interviewed are neither the first, nor will they be the last, to encounter something that might be called supernatural. Since time immemorial, ghosts have haunted novels, plays, and religious texts, and thousands around the world have claimed to see them or sense their eerie presence.

I vividly remember one afternoon in 2016, in a house in the village of Wolvercote, when I saw something that I still can't explain. A heavy, laminated map lifted itself off a hanging nail and flew two metres across the room, decapitating my housemate's Buddha statue in the process, I didn't imagine it, the damage was plain to see.

It was a bit like a parody of David Warner's famously sticky end in *The Omen*.

To this day my former house mate still thinks I had a wild party which led to the beheading of his statue, I have no explanation for it, I'm simply reporting what I witnessed, it was far too heavy to have been blown two metres across the room by a gust of wind, many people still don't believe me, but to quote the theme tune of the BBC show *Uncanny*, "I know what I saw".

Perhaps my latent Catholicism somehow telepathically compelled the map to slice off the statue's head in a moment of divine overreaction, or was it the ghost from the now defunct paper mill which once stood behind the house, long dead, but outraged by the use of plastic to laminate an antique map, long dead… but awake.

We may never uncover the full truth behind the many mysterious accounts in this book. For me, it has been a fascinating journey, and I hope you—the reader, whether believer or not—have enjoyed this expedition into Oxford's spectral realm.

SELECT BIBLIOGRAPHY

Christine Hartweg Amy Robsart: A Life and Its End
First published in 2017
Copyright © 2017 Christine Hartweg
ISBN 978-1548783600

Betty Puttick Oxfordshire: Stories of the Supernatural
published 2003
© Betty Puttick 2003
COUNTRYSIDE BOOKS
3 Catherine Road Newbury, Berkshire
ISBN 1 85306 811 X

John Richardson Ghost Stories of Oxford and County
J Hannon & Co Publishers
ISBN 13-9780904233179...

Marilyn Yurdan Unexplained Oxford and Oxfordshire
First published October 2002 by
The Book Castle
12 Church Street
Dunstable
Bedfordshire LU5 4RU
ISBN 1 903747 21

LIST OF ILLUSTRATIONS AND PHOTOGRAPHS

Chapter 1.
Passageway in the house on Holywell Street where the skeleton was discovered.
{Photograph} Tom McDonnell

The living room in the haunted guest house.
{Photograph} Tom McDonnell

Chapter 3.
The window paned door in Jesus College, which the mysterious man hid behind.
{Photograph} Tom McDonnell

Chapter 5.
The Unicorn Theatre, a pretty place with a troublesome spirit.
{Photograph} Tom McDonnell

Chapter 6.
The haunted Bear Inn, possibly Oxfords oldest pub.
{Photograph} Tom McDonnell

Chapter 7.
Oliver Shaw performing at the Tomohawk Xmas party in the Cellar 2002, being watched by a punter who seemingly has no eyes.
{Photograph} Tom McDonnell

Chapter 8.
Jun, outside staircase 13.
{Photograph} Tom McDonnell

Jun looking up to his haunted room.
{Photograph} Tom McDonnell

Chapter 9.
Magpie Lane
By Gus Mills

Chapter 10.
Wadham College, Oxford
By Gus Mills

Chapter 12.
The Monk's Bar and the Grandfather Clock at the Chequers—a pub where, according to a barmaid in September 2025, glasses have been known to mysteriously fly off the shelves.
(Photograph) Tom McDonnell

Chapter 13.
The Ruins of Godstow
{Photograph} Tom McDonnell

Chapter 14.
The Trout Inn, a contender for being Oxfords most haunted pub.
{Photograph} Tom McDonnell

Chapter 17.
The Saxon Tower, Oxfords oldest building.
{Photograph} Tom McDonnell

Chapter 23.
A memorial to the founder of Trinity college, Thomas Pope and his third wife, but are they really resting in peace?
{Photograph} Tom McDonnell

Chapter 24.
The Memorial to Amy Robsart in the church she is said to wander.
{Photograph} Tom McDonnell

Lady Dudley's Pond in Cumnor, said to never freeze, is rumoured to hold the spirit of Amy Robsart.
{Photograph} Tom McDonnell

Chapter 25.
Paying my respects to Kenneth Grahame and Mouse.
{Photograph} by Kirk G Ellingham

Chapter 29
Asher Dust conjuring up some musical magic at the Jericho Tavern.
{Photograph} Tom McDonnell

Chapter 32.
Evening in Radcliffe Square
By Gus Mills

Chapter 34.
Jordon, back at the Oxford Castle, around a decade after helping with an interesting paranormal hunt.
{Photograph} Tom McDonnell

Chapter 35.
The Divinity School, the haunt of the limping pot boy.
{Photograph} Tom McDonnell

Chapter 37.
Tolkien with Pipe
By Jon Patterson

Chapter 39.
The Site of Napier's Execution.
{Photograph} Tom McDonnell

Chapter 40.
Graves of men who may hold secrets.
{Photograph} Tom McDonnell

Chapter 43.
The effigy of John Crocker.
{Photograph} Iain Stevenson

Chapter 47.
St Giles Graveyard, home to the ghost of the sobbing Lady
{Photograph} Tom McDonnell

ACKNOWLEDGEMENTS AND CREDITS

I must give a lot of credit to Marilyn Yurdan, Nuala Young, Iain Stevenson, Magnus Macfarlane and Eva Wagner who specifically asked me to put the ghosts to rest and publish her and Nuala's research notes.

I am very grateful to Susannah Cartwright for her support and to the general editors, Marmaduke Postlethwaite and Joe Wilkins.

A massive thanks to the photographer Kirk G Ellingham and to the artists Jon Patterson and Gus Mills, whose fantastic website is definitely worth checking out at www.gusmillsgallery.co.uk. And of course, a big thanks to all of those brave people who submitted their tales of terror.

ENDNOTES

1. Braiker Brian, Christopher Hitchens at His Most Polemic The Guardian 16 December 2011
Christopher Hitchens provocative words on death

2. Sloan Liam, Experts Reveal Brutal Viking Massacre, The Oxford Mail 05 November 2010
The slaying of Danish settlers in Oxford

3. Holloway Stu and Carrie Personal correspondence December 2016 The fascinating accounts of the ghost in the Holywell Street guesthouse

4. Sanchari and Rohan personal correspondence 28/08/2024, The strange shadowy figure on St Mary's passage.

5. Alfie W.H and Alfie C Personal correspondence 29/07/2021 The two Alfie's disturbing experience with the man behind the door

6. Flint Peter, Dalton Terence R.A.F Kenley www.kenleyrevival.org Accounts of the so called "Hardest Day"
Originally published 1985

7. …Stevenson Iain: Personal correspondence 06/06/2023 - The strange story of the bizarre room service at the Randolph

8. Kitching Alan The Pleasant Historie of The Unicorn Theatre by its Onlie Begetter © Friends of Abingdon Unicorn Theatre 2017 The history and concept behind the Unicorn Theatre

9. NIchol Mikey Personal Correspondence 09/05/2025 The Unicorn Theatre poltergeist

10. THE Conduit Ghost Faringdon Advertiser and Vale of the White Horse Gazette - Saturday 22 September 1888 page 5
Content provided by THE BRITISH LIBRARY BOARD. ALL RIGHTS RESERVED Reports of the sensational Conduit Ghost

11. Abingdon A Ghost Scare Henley Advertiser - Saturday 20 June 1891 Page 5 of 8 Content provided by THE BRITISH LIBRARY BOARD. ALL RIGHTS RESERVED The return of the violent Abingdon ghost

12. Young Nuala Wagner Eva, Ghost and Gore research notes The Bear had an 8th century graveyard below, 08/05/94

13. Wagner Eva: Personal Correspondence 06/04/2024 Eva and the strange accounts of the grey man at The Bear

14. Chief Mr Personal Correspondence 04/05/2024 Chiefs fascinating account of the

old Cellar {then called the Corn Dolly] nightclubs poltergeist

15　Higginbotham Peter www.workhouses.org.uk Oxford, Oxfordshire Up to 1834 Copyright 2025 The fascinating history of Oxfords workhouse and house of correction, and the Mayor of Oxfords complaints.

16　Sang Jun Chun Personal experience 08/05/2018 Juns account of the visitations he experienced.

17　Kruglikova Nina Personal Correspondence 10/12/2020 Nina told me about St Aldates once being the Jewish section of Oxford

18　The College in War Time https://www.pmb.ox.ac.uk/college-war-time Pembroke hosted members of the School of Military Aeronautics in war time

19　Oxford Journal -published Saturday 14 February 1852 Page 3. Death notice in local paper of Eliza Burill

20　Sang Jun Chun Personal correspondence 08/05/2018 Juns fascinating account of his time at Pembroke and his unique childhood experiences.

21　Barbara Personal Correspondence 2015, A former bank clerk informed of several Prudence's tricks

22　Yurdan Marilyn Personal Correspondence 11/08/2025 Marilyn's friend heard footsteps at the bank -accompanied by the shuffling of a dress.

23　Darryl -Personal Correspondence 29/09/2023, Darryls reports of Prudence Burcote's ghost

24　Wagner Eva: Personal Correspondence 18/12/2023 Eva's meeting with the bank manager and his accounts of Prudence and the strange story of the American visitors and the Puritan maid

25　McDonnell Tom Sweete Wittie Soules Published by Autolycus Books 2016 P.55 John London's remarks on the ruinous state of the Austin Friary in Oxford

26　Oxford and County Ghost Stories Collected by John Richardson Copyright: J. RICHARDSON 1977. Published by Hannon (Publishers) Oxford 30 Great Clarendon Street, Oxford, England. P.9 – 10 The accounts of ghostly monks collected by John Richardson

27　The Liverpool Echo and evening Express. Monday, June 19th 1967. page 7 The strange poisoning case at Wadham

28　Puttick Betty Oxfordshire: Stories of the Supernatural
Published 2003 by Countryside Books, P.29-30, The 1960's reports of ghosts at Wadham

29　Taylor and Kayla Personal Correspondence 14/07/2019 The two American summer school students' surreal experiences at Wadham

30 Oxford and County Ghost Stories Collected by John Richardson Copyright: J. RICHARDSON 1977
    Published by Hannon) Oxford 30 Great Clarendon Street, Oxford, England. P.10
    The oppressive forces at work in the Porters lodge

31 …C reaser Personal correspondence 04/11/2023 Two mysterious presences in a house on Linton Road

32 O'Brien Gary Personal Correspondence 21/08/2023 The mysterious spirit on Linton Road, which hid O'Briens Key

33 Walters Rob, Richardson Dave, The Oxford Drinker Mitre set to become Gusto Italian Restaurant Published June 2022 A frustrating modernisation of one of Oxfords classic pubs

34 Ann Godson Julie https://www.facebook.com/julieanngodson 21/12/2023 Godson's superb history Facebook page provides a fascinating insight into the last hours of Eunice's life

35 Young Nuala, Wagner Eva, Ghost and Gore Research Notes . 08/05/1994 The legend of the monk and the grandfather clock at the Chequers

36 Flantzer Susan Rosamund De Clifford, Mistress of Henry II, King of England. www.unofficialroyalty.com Published October 5 2020 Rosamond's education and affair with the King, and the complications of the Kings relationship with Eleanor.

37 Evans T Zteve The Legend of Fair Rosamund https:ztevetevans.wordpress.com Published 02/08/2016 The many ways Rosamund is believed to have died at the hands of Eleanor

38 Thacker Fred, The Stripling Thames
    Published 1909, The legend of Rosamond's supernatural transformation

39 Flantzer Susan Rosamund De Clifford, Mistress of Henry II, King of England. www.unofficialroyalty.com Published October 5 2020
    Rosamond's Tomb and the Bishop of Lincolns reaction

40 Clark Ira Samuel Daniel's Complaint of Rosamond Renaissance Quarterly Vol 23. No 2 {Summer 1970} pages 152-162 published by Cambridge University Press, A study of the Elizabethan poet Samuel Daniels Complaint of Rosamund

41 Bauman Thomas Rosamunde www.Oxfordmusiconline.com
    Published 01/12/1992 The details of Schweitzer's Singspiel, inspired by a story in Joseph Addison's Spectator

42 Luraghi Silvia An Undeservedly Forgotten Score www.theoperacritic.com Published November 2016, A critique of Donizetti's little-known tribute to Rosamond of England.

43 Munod-Dupont Clara The Revolt Published by Quercus 2018 ISBN 1529402905 Rosamond's latest literary appearance

44 Sillince Heather. Personal Correspondence: 13/09/ 2022 Heathers fascinating and detailed account of her time at the Trout.

45 The Oxford Journal - Saturday 27 February 1886 page 8, The death of Shonberg

46 Bathing Fatality at Black Jack's Hole Oxfordshire Weekly News - Wednesday 23 July 1890
Content provided by THE BRITISH LIBRARY BOARD. ALL RIGHTS RESERVED. Reginald's tragic death

47 Manchester Courier Page 2 Published Wednesday 23 December 1908 Alice's mysterious death

48 Servant Girl Drowned. Tragedy of Black Jack's Hole Oxford Chronicle and Reading Gazette
Page 8 published Friday 19th December 1919 . Nellie Hubbocks death

49 Siddle John The Daily Mail : Oxford University Student, 19, Who Drowned in river while celebrating the end of exams Published 23/07/2024 A very sad recent case of drowning near Black Jacks.

50 Richardson John Ghost Stories of Oxford and County J Hannon & Co Publishers ISBN 13-9780904233179… 1977 P 36 The legend of the Drunken Sailors suicide.

51 Thacker S Fred The Stripling Thames, A Book of the River Above Oxford, published 1909
The legend of the evil Goblin of Black Jack's Hole

52 Yurdan Marilyn, Unexplained Oxford and Oxfordshire, P63
The strange account of the Port Meadow spectre

53 Young Nuala, Wagner Eva - Edited by Macfarlane Magnus Ghost Stories 1 Personal Research notes 22/02/2022 The strange story of the Lincoln college organist

54 Young Nuala, Wagner Eva - Edited by Macfarlane Magnus, Ghost Stories 1 Personal Research notes 22/02/2022 The suffocating presence in Lincoln college bar and the employee who felt the wrath of the spectre's

55 Iovino Joe https://www.umc. published on September 20, 2016
The Wesley room and the mocking nicknames given to the Methodists

56 Rutterford Paul Personal correspondence 02/12/2023 Paul notified me of the legend of the shaking table in the Wesley Room

57 Raynor Shane Ghosts, Supernaturalism and the Wesley Poltergeist www.ministrymatters.com The Wesley families encounter with the Epworth poltergeist

58 Ballard Simon Personal Correspondence 04/08/2025 Simon informed of the exchange his colleague had with the medium who was spooked by a ghost on the

stairs of the Saxon tower

59 Sahana personal correspondence 09/08/2024 Strange visitations at the Eastgate Hotel.

60 Yurdan Marilyn, Unexplained Oxford and Oxfordshire ISBN 1 90374721 X Published by the Book Castle October 2022 P.22-24 An overview of paranormal activity documented by Marilyn Yurdan in her book on unexplained Oxford

61 Yurdan Marilyn Personal correspondence November 2022 The post 1984 ghost reports collected by Marilyn Yurdan

62 ' Heaney P Personal correspondence 08/01/2023 Strange incidents in P Heaney's former house

63 Yurdan Marilyn, Unexplained Oxford and Oxfordshire ISBN 1 90374721 X Published by the Book Castle October 2022 The strange encounter between the Playhouse cleaner and the white spectre

64 Image Simon Personal Correspondence 02/03/2023, Local historian, Simon Image was very helpful in providing information about the history of Beaumont Palace

65 Wagner Eva, Personal Correspondence 18/12/2023, Eva makes a valid point about the problems of identifying ghosts in Oxford, due to the clothes worn by holy men and students.

66 Burge Paul, Personal Correspondence, 2013 The mysterious scent of an invisible woman in the Playhouse Theatre.

67 Young Nuala, Wagner Eva GHOST (& GORE) TOUR Notes from 08-5-94, Nuala and Eva's notes from the early 1990s, on ghosts and the paranormal, the poltergeist of St Edmund Hall

68 Mann Darren https://www.paranormaldatabase.com/hotspots/oxford.php The paranormal database has added the legend of the hanging boy at St Edmund's, although it's unlikely we will ever discover his identity Copyright 2025

69 Jaffey J. M St Edmund Hall Magazine 1951-52...Published on Oct 1, 1951 The students of St Edmund produced interesting essays on the occult in the early 1950's

70 Davies Nick. The Guardian. Father Jeremy Davies, Obituary 08/12/2022 A candid view of the Exorcist's life from the perspective of his nephew

71 Exorcist warned of the dangers of yoga, acupuncture and horoscopes The Sydney Morning Herald Published 11/01/2023 Father Davies interesting views on alternative medicine

72 Davies Nick. The Guardian. Father Jeremy Davies, Obituary 08/12/2022 The nephew of Father Davies had a very different outlook on life

73 Russel the Trinity Archivist- Personal correspondence October 2020 The strange phantom footsteps and sightings of the lady in the tower

74 Warton Thomas: The Life of Sir Thomas Pope: founder of Trinity College Oxford. Chiefly compiled from original evidences. With an appendix of papers, never before printed. The second edition, corrected and enlarged P.188- 189, Popes honourable intentions behind the establishment of Trinity college and the irony of Thomas Cranmer facilitating a Catholic wedding.

75 Warton Thomas: The Life of Sir Thomas Pope: founder of Trinity College Oxford. Chiefly compiled from original evidence. With an appendix of papers, never before printed. The second edition, corrected and enlarged P.190-192, Powlett's heroic endeavours

76 Warton Thomas: The Life of Sir Thomas Pope: founder of Trinity College Oxford. Chiefly compiled from original evidences. With an appendix of papers, never before printed. The second edition, corrected and enlarged P 194-197, Dame Emily's responsibilities at the college were unusual for a woman of her time, the students who were admitted during her tenure spoke very highly of her

77 Warton Thomas: The Life of Sir Thomas Pope: founder of Trinity College Oxford. Chiefly compiled from original evidences. With an appendix of papers, never before printed. The second edition, corrected and enlarged P.199, Dame Emily's order to destroy the glass she had commissioned, the order to destroy was likely due to superstitious fears

78 Warton Thomas: The Life of Sir Thomas Pope: founder of Trinity College Oxford. Chiefly compiled from original evidences. With an appendix of papers, never before printed. The second edition, corrected and enlarged…The life and times of Dame Emily

79 Davis Jules personal correspondence 16/04/2024 Strange goings on in the Wardens room at Trinity college

80 Image Simon Personal Correspondence 08/10/2012 Local Historian Simon Image presented his version of events leading to Amy's death

81 Christine Hartweg Amy Robsart: A Life and Its EndFirst published in 2017 Copyright © 2017 Christine Hartweg ISBN 978-1548783600
P.78 Hartwegs argument against Amy Roberts suicide

82 Christine Hartweg Amy Robsart: A Life and Its End First published in 2017 Copyright © 2017 Christine Hartweg ISBN 978-1548783600 Hartwegs argument against Amy Roberts suicide P.59 – 60 The details of Amy Robsart's funeral

83 Christine Hartweg Amy Robsart: A Life and Its End First published in 2017 Copyright © 2017 Christine Hartweg ISBN 978-1548783600 P143-p144 The fire at St Mary's church

84 Image Simon Personal Correspondence 2012 Simon informed me for the legend

of the choir boys witnessing Amy's apparition.

85   Marion www.tripadvisor.com 18 August 2013 Marion had an interesting stay at The Bear and Ragged Staff.

86   Dale Adam Personal correspondence 05/08/2025-09/08/2025 Adam told me about the strange atmosphere of his childhood home in Wytham Abbey and the rumour of the bannisters having been taken from Amy Robart's place, I discovered a few days later that there was probably some truth to the rumour.

87   Puttick Betty Oxfordshire- Stories of the Supernatural Countryside Books 2003 P.34-P.35 Lady Dudley's pond and the Death of Robert Dudley

88   Christine Hartweg Amy Robsart: A Life and Its End First published in 2017 Copyright © 2017 Christine Hartweg ISBN 978-1548783600 P.68 John Airds theory on Amy's death.

89   Holloway Stuart Personal Correspondence The legend of Alistair Grahames headless ghost wandering around Holywell cemetery. December 2021.

90   Evening Irish Times - Friday 30 October 1908 Image © THE BRITISH LIBRARY BOARD. ALL RIGHTS RESERVED. Page 9 A not particularly positive review of Grahame's most famous book

91   Oxford Chronicle and Reading Gazette - Friday 23 October 1908 Image © THE BRITISH LIBRARY BOARD. ALL RIGHTS RESERVED. Another lukewarm review for Wind in the Willows

92   Jones LeAnne Jessica. Cedars, S.R. ed. https://www.gradesaver.com/the-wind-in-the-willows/study-guide/the-painful-history-of-mouse in MLA Format 25 August 2014 Web. 7 November 2023. The Wind in the Willows the Painful History of "Mouse. The theories behind the creation of Mister Toad and the characters possible influence on the authors son. GradeSaver

93   Mount Harry The Daily Mail How the genius behind Wind in the Willows drove the son who inspired him to suicide November 2010, updated 26 Nov 2010 The grim death of Alistair Grahame

94   Mount Harry How the Genius Behind Wind in the Willows Drove the Son Who inspired Him to Suicide The Daily Mail November 2010, updated 26 Nov 2010... How Alistair Grahame's death inspired special provisions for disabled students at Oxfird

95   Ramona: Personal Correspondence 15/04/2024, Ramona's interesting accounts of the paranormal at the palace.

96   Mr O Personal correspondence. 12/07/2022The fascinating tale of the mysterious entity at the door of a lodgings building on the grounds of Blenheim Palace

97   Ricketts, Rita (2012) "International Dateline: The Butcher, The Baker, the Candlestick Maker," Against the Grain: Vol. 24: Iss. 3, Article 39 Benjamin

Blackwells perception of Bliss Court

98 Fisher Nigel Personal correspondence 13/06/2025 The floating figure near Wytham Woods

99 Nichol Mikey personal correspondence 09/05/2025 The reports of the Jericho Tavern poltergeist.

100 Sha-Hembury Jordon Personal correspondence 18/08/2025 The ghostly going ons at St Clare's.

101 City and County News ; A Belgian Appeal for Land Oxford Chronicle and Reading Gazette - Friday 9 March 1917 Page 12 The Belgian woman's mission to help with the war effort.

102 Theft From a Pantry Oxford Chronicle and Reading Gazette - Friday 31 December 1909 Page 12 Content provided by THE BRITISH LIBRARY BOARD. ALL RIGHTS A quantity of food was stolen from the house in 1909.

103 Shaw Personal correspondence 18/08/2025 A police officers thoughts on my "inside job" theory regarding the pantry crime

104 Mav Personal correspondence 18/08/2025 Speculation as to why the thieves didn't steal anything but food.

105 Warbourton Personal correspondence 18/08/2025 The criminal sociologist's interesting "testing the water" theory

106 Sha-Hembury Jordon Personal correspondence 18/08/2025 Jordon's information that a person could indeed fit in the old servery hatch at St Clare's.

107 Young Nuala, Wagner Eva Ghost and Gore Notes 8/04/1994 Reports of strange happenings in the New Theatre

108 Walter {aka Widge} Personal Correspondence The amusing story of Bowie and the bouquet . 1998

109 Wagner Eva Personal Correspondence 24/05/2024 Eva's account of the haunted ex policeman

110 Norman M Personal correspondence 28/12/2023 The Exeter students follow up tale on the fallen student, and their rather relaxed attitude to death in the later 1940's.

111 Stevenson Iain Personal correspondence May 2024 The legend of Dish-washing Mary

112 Spencer Dan, The Escape of the Empress Matilda from Oxford Castle in 1142 www.Danspencerinfo.com Published 2018, The incredible escape of Empress Matilda

113 Kronenwetter, Michael). Capital punishment: a reference handbook. ABC-CLIO. p. 172. ISBN 978-1-57607-432-9 2010 Woods's record of Ketch's work in Oxford

114 Jordan Sha-Hembury personal correspondence, 2020 Jordon kindly provided me with his personal account of the castle ghosts

115 Kilcoyne Angel 02/07/2025 Personal correspondence, Angela's fascinating account of her brush with the undead at Oxford Castle

116 Goodger Amanda: Personal Correspondence 24/07/2025 Amanda's fascinating account of her visits to Oxford Castle and Prison.

117 Cornell Martyn Zythophile.co.uk The Potboy in History, Literature and Art 17/09/2007
Cornel's award-winning blog brings to life the role of the potboy, and the entertaining words of the Reverend Charles Maurice

118 Young Nuala, Wagner Eva- edited by Macfarlane Magnus, Ghost Story Research Notes 22/02/2022 The legend of the Divinity School Potboy

119 Sault Keith and Sharman Laura : Personal Correspondence 2008. The Mystery of the two men in Chatham Road.

120 Image Simon Personal Correspondence May 2007 Simon informed me of Matt's positive perception of a room which had a grisly history

121 Goodger Amanda Personal correspondence 24/07/2024 Amanda's fascinating theories on Vibes and Frequencies

122 Wagner Eva, personal correspondence- Eva told me that Tolkien. In later life, permanently has a pipe lodged in his mouth 27/04/2024

123 Ross Will Tolkien's Ghost at Merton College https://www.darkoxfordshire.co.uk/explore/tolkiens-ghost-at-merton-college/ Published 01/12/2021 Ross has written an entertaining article on Tolkien's ghost on his excellent website darkoxfordshire.co.uk Co Copyright 2025. All Rights Reserved Dark Oxfordshire. Copyright 2025.

124 Young Nuala Wagner Eva, Ghost and Gore research notes The Bear had an 8th century graveyard below, 08/05/94 The slurping sounds at the Black Drum inn

125 Glasgow Herald reports Saturday 17 June 1871 page 5 English Bankrupts The landlord of the Black Drummers bankruptcy problems

126 Serious Fire in Pembroke Street Oxford Oxford Chronicle and Reading Gazette - Saturday 25 March 1899 Content provided by THE BRITISH LIBRARY BOARD. ALL RIGHTS RESERVED. The Mysterious blaze at Pembroke street

127 Whitehead John, Personal Correspondence, Whitehead, a Catholic scholar informed of the blessing of the site of Napier's execution. May 2019

128 Young Nuala, Ghost and Gore Research Notes
08-05-1994, Nuala's research notes inform us of the legend regards to Napier's bones and their possible internment in France, the country where he was ordained.

129 Puttick Betty Oxfordshire- Stories of the Supernatural
Countryside Books 2003 P.28 Napier's ghost at Magdalen

130 Young Nuala, Ghost and Gore Research Notes 08-05-1994 Nula's notes on the frightening legend of Napier's carriage

131 Richardson John Ghost Stories of Oxford and County J Hannon & Co Publishers ISBN 13-9780904233179… 1977 P.35-The strange account of Simon Kent and Jane Smith

132 Hughes Pete Oxford Mail Remember When: 500-Year-Old Hotel was Demolished by Woolworths
Published April 20th 2019

133 Shahnazi Bahram Personal Correspondence 27/07/2025 Bahram first alerted me to the Legend of George, the resident ghost of Boswells.

134 Prew Sally Personal correspondence 27/07/2025 Sally directed me towards some of the events which scared the staff of Boswells

135 Shahnazi Bahram Personal Correspondence 27/07/2025 The account of the stock room manager who was too scared to enter a certain section of the stockroom

136 Morris Tony Martyrs Cross https://morrisoxford.co.uk Copyright 2025 | MORRIS OXFORD All rights reserved Morris Tony Morris provides a fascinating take on the execution of the Martyrs in his fantastic website

137 Image Simon Personal Correspondence 04/01/2022 local historian Simon Image's take on the infamous executions.

138 Ballard Simon, Morris Tony Martyrs Cross https://morrisoxford.co.uk Copyright 2025 | MORRIS OXFORD All rights reserved Morris Simon Ballard's interesting take on the site of the martyr's execution- and the platform from which Cranmer was forced to watch his friends perish.

139 Ballard Simon Personal correspondence 04/08/2025 Simon's views on the so-called Devils Tower

140 Swarbrick Nick Personal Correspondence 17/12/2023 the legend of the boy with the lantern

141 Doyle Richard Personal Correspondence Summer 2015, The best-selling author of thrillers, the late Richard Doyle, informed of this quirky tradition at his old college.

142 Wood Thomas On Staircase Six Exeter College Association Register 2002 P.26 Woods account of the ghost of John Crocker

143 Richards Elizabeth. An Essex Man Wrote the Song Made Famous by Aussies in the Dessert. The Essex Newsman Herald., published 21/11/1950 Woods arrangement of Waltzing Matilda gained huge popularity
144 Ward Russell Dr Thomas-Wood Biography Part 11 Bures.org.uk, Published 06/11/2011 the many achievements of Dr Thomas Wood

145 Stevenson Iain Personal Correspondence 09/07/2025 The rumour concerning a former chaplains dislike of the statue's presence.

146 New Milton Advertiser - Saturday 27 December 1958 page 6 Image © Iliffe News & Media Ltd. Image created courtesy of THE BRITISH LIBRARY BOARD. Source material for "the gentlest ghost"

147 Alysa Landry Native History: Cook Explores Hawaiian Islands, Brings TB, Indiancountrytoday.com Published 13 September 2018, How the indigenous people of Hawaii mistook Captain Cook and his men to be Gods and Cooks demise.

148 Bolden Mark Personal correspondence December 2018 Marks unusual encounter at the museum

149 Adams Geraldine Kendall Pitt Rivers Museum removes shrunken heads from display after ethical review Published 18 September 2020. Museumsassociatian.org

150 Young Nuala, Wagner Eve Ghost Route Notes 7/05/1994 Notes on the hauntings of St John's college.

151 Richardson John Ghost Stories of Oxford and County J Hannon & Co Publishers ISBN 13-9780904233179… 1977 P 35—36 Mr Parker's Grandfather's account of the Grey Lady

Dead but Awake

www.ingramcontent.com/pod-product-compliance
Lightning Source LLC
Chambersburg PA
CBHW050327010526
44119CB00050B/708